YOU ARE
YOUR BEST
THING

EDITED BY

TARANA BURKE

AND

BRENÉ BROWN

RANDOM HOUSE

NEW YORK

YOU ARE YOUR BEST THING

VULNERABILITY, SHAME RESILIENCE, AND THE BLACK EXPERIENCE

AN ANTHOLOGY

Published in the United States by Random House,
an imprint and division of Penguin Random House LLC, New York.

RANDOM HOUSE and the HOUSE colophon are registered
trademarks of Penguin Random House LLC.

Contributor credits begin on page 221.

LIBRARY OF CONGRESS CATALOGING-IN-PUBLICATION DATA

NAMES: Burke, Tarana, editor. | Brown, Brené, editor.
TITLE: You are your best thing : vulnerability, shame resilience,
and the black experience / edited by Tarana Burke and Brené Brown.
Description: New York : Random House, 2021.
IDENTIFIERS: LCCN 2020057201 (print) | LCCN 2020057202 (ebook) |
ISBN 9780593243626 (hardback) | ISBN 9780593243640 (ebook)
SUBJECTS: LCSH: Shame. | Resilience (Personality trait) |
Vulnerability (Personality trait) | Blacks—Social conditions.
CLASSIFICATION: LCC BF575.S45 Y68 2021 (print) |
LCC BF575.S45 (ebook) | DDC 152.4/4—dc23
LC record available at https://lccn.loc.gov/2020057201
LC ebook record available at https://lccn.loc.gov/2020057202

Printed in the United States of America on acid-free paper

randomhousebooks.com

987654321

"Sethe," he says, "me and you, we got more yesterday than anybody. We need some kind of tomorrow."

He leans over and takes her hand. With the other he touches her face. "You your best thing, Sethe. You are." His holding fingers are holding hers.

"Me? Me?"

—TONI MORRISON, *Beloved*

CONTENTS

INTRODUCTION: A CONVERSATION

BRENÉ BROWN: We could start the story of this book when you texted me to ask if we could talk, and I thought you wanted to continue our ongoing conversation about wallpaper and landscaping—but what came before that? When did the idea for this book come to you?

TARANA BURKE: It was after we did #SharetheMic on social media, in the summer of 2020. There had been this intense public unrest happening in the country after George Floyd and Breonna Taylor were murdered. In private, I was having these really heartfelt conversations with Black folks who were just struggling: *I can't watch any more of this. I can't take this anymore. I cannot . . .* And in public, the conversation was, *How can we get white people to be better? How can we get white people to be antiracist?* Antiracism became the order of the day. But there was no focus on Black humanity. I kept thinking, *Where's the space for us to talk about what this does to us, how this affects our lives?* And so I was thinking to myself that I really wanted to have a conversation with you.

At first, I struggled to text you. I kept asking myself, *Why am I hesitating to reach out to her? We have a close enough friendship to talk about anything.* Your work is so important to me and my experience as a human being, but as a Black woman, I often felt like I had to contort myself to fit into the work and see myself in it. I wanted to talk to you about adding to it: "What is the Black experience with shame resilience?" Because white supremacy has added another layer to the kind of shame we have to deal with, and the kind of resilience we have to build, and the kind of vulnerability that we are constantly subjected to whether we choose it or not.

So, yeah, I called and said all of that—but I was not as eloquent [*laughter*] at the time. I will never forget that phone call. I texted, *Can we talk?* and you texted back, *Sure.* Once we got on the phone and I shared the idea, the first thing you said was "Oh, hell yeah. Oh, absolutely! Yes, I want to talk about that. Yes, I want to do this." At that point I was just thinking, *Oh, and here I was worrying about offending you and wanting to have a real conversation.* So, that was the beginning from my side. What was happening on your side?

BRENÉ: From my side, well, admittedly, I'd probably do anything you ask me to do. But the timing was bigger than us. I had really been grappling over the last couple of years with trying to figure out how to be more inclusive—how to present the work in a way that invited more people to see themselves. The last thing I ever wanted to do was put work in the world around shame, vulnerability, and courage, then make people feel like they had to do something extra to find themselves in it. I thought I had controlled for that with my sample, because I've always been hypervigilant about diversity in the people I interview and in data sources. In fact, one of the early criticisms of my work was that the sample population actually overindexed around Black women and Latinx folks. But I started to get comments, especially from Black women and men: "I had to work at it more to see myself in it than I would have preferred or I would have liked to or than I even should have had to." Finally, it was the combination of a conversation with you and a conversation with Austin Channing Brown on her TV show, where I thought, *The problem isn't the research. The research resonates with a diverse group of people because it's based on a diverse sample. But the way I present my research to the world does* not *always resonate because I often use myself and my stories as examples, and I have a very privileged white experience.* That was the huge aha for me.

TARANA: Yeah, that makes sense.

BRENÉ: One of the things that struck me was, in *The Gifts of Imperfection*, there's a scene where I'm in sweats and have dirty hair and I'm running up the Nordstrom escalator with my daughter to exchange some shoes that her grandmother bought her. Immediately, I'm overwhelmed because I look and feel like shit, and there's all these perfect-looking people giving me the side-eye. Just as I start to go into some shame, a pop song starts playing and Ellen breaks out into the robot. I mean full-on, unfiltered, unaware—just sheer joy. As the perfect people start staring at her, I'm reduced to this moment where I have to decide, *Am I going to betray her and roll my eyes and say, "Ellen, settle down," or am I just going to let her do her thing—let her be joyful and un- ashamed?* I end up choosing her and actually dancing with her. It's a great story about choosing my daughter over ac- ceptance by strangers, but I've shopped with enough Black friends to know that if I was not dressed up—even if I was dressed up—and I was in a department store and my Black daughter broke into a dance, there would be a whole other set of variables to consider. Including being hassled by secu- rity, possibly separated from my daughter, even arrested. So when you asked me if we could focus the work through the lens of the Black experience, it was a "hell yes" from me. I want to figure out how to better serve. In addition to telling my story, which I think is helpful, I want to co-create so peo- ple see themselves in this work. Co-creation is how we can tell stories from the Black experience that illustrate the data. Does that make sense?

TARANA: It does. This is our first time really digging into your grappling with this. Your questions make absolute sense, and it also makes sense why you wanted to do this together. You still said, "Are you sure you want me to do it with you? You have my permission to use my work and do it."

BRENÉ: I was scared. I'm still scared.

TARANA: I get it. I understand the fear, and I know we have to be prepared for the question about you being an editor of a book about Black experience. But there's nobody I trust more, particularly on these topics, who has studied them more and who cares more. It's not just the research piece—there are other people who study these topics. But you combine the research expertise with compassion. You are—this sounds really corny—an embodiment of your work, of the research, of the knowledge. I think it takes the eye of somebody who has done the level of research you have done and who cares about other people's stories. I feel such a sense of responsibility and protectiveness about the stories we've asked people to share for this anthology. We have to be good stewards of this information. So I definitely get the fear and reluctance, but I believe good stewardship takes both of us. I know as we read these powerful essays, we both took turns feeling a little overwhelmed with the responsibility of protecting them.

BRENÉ: I've been doing this work for twenty-five years now. I know the stories in this book can change—even save—people's lives. It's an honor to do this with you. I've been a shame and vulnerability researcher for a long time, but not any longer than you have been an expert in the work. You have been teaching and training this work for decades. We both used the word "shame" long before most people could stomach it. They were experiencing it, of course. But we were naming it before most people were willing to do that.

TARANA: I just remember this feeling washing over me, again and again, and thinking: *This shame is gonna kill us. This shame is gonna kill us.* Being at family gatherings, being at cultural gatherings, watching the young people I worked with, knowing what they were like in our private spaces when they were open and free, and then watching them in public spaces and saying, "Oh my gosh, this is going to kill us." And then this idea of shame resilience added another "Aha," because my first thought was, *Oh, but shame hasn't killed us yet.* Then I started asking myself, *Why hasn't it?* I've learned it's because there's this powerful resilience that we've tapped into but have yet to name.

BRENÉ: Yes! And my hope is that co-creating this anthology with these incredible storytellers and writers helps us name it. There is one thing that I think is important to clarify about our process of working together—especially for other researchers and creators who are thinking, *Okay, but how does co-creation actually work?* For starters, I wouldn't have done the book without you agreeing to be the first author.

TARANA: I didn't understand that at all at first, but I get it now.

BRENÉ: Here's what we need to understand: In co-creation, lived experience always trumps academic experience.

TARANA: I don't know. Is that a rule, like an academic rule?

BRENÉ: No. It should be. It's definitely my rule.

TARANA: I was about to say, that has to be a Brené rule, because I don't know that all academics would agree. But I agree that you can't make your research useful to people, accessible to people, if you don't prioritize lived experience, relevance, and accessibility.

BRENÉ: Lived experience has got to take the lead. Unquestionably. And in co-creation projects, lived experience should not only take the authorship lead, it should take a financial lead where it can, which is why all of my proceeds from this book are going back to storytellers in the Black community.

TARANA: When I think about our co-creating, the construct that I didn't fully grasp until I read your book was vulnerability and the role it plays in our lives. My lived experience told me that the entire idea and experience of vulnerability feels like a very dangerous place to play, an unsafe thing to even consider or think about as a Black person in this country. As I read your work about vulnerability being the foundation of courage and the birthplace of love and joy and trust—these are the places that didn't fit. I was forced to contort myself and try to understand my reaction of, *Oh, no. Vulnerability means something very different to me.* That was a big learning for me—just naming vulnerability and talking about it and thinking about it.

BRENÉ: This is the bones of it. I believe the greatest casualty of trauma—including white supremacy, which is definitely a form of intergenerational systemic trauma—is that vulnerability becomes dangerous, risky, even life-threatening. But here's the painful piece—it's not like if you're Black, you don't need vulnerability to experience joy, belonging, intimacy, and love. It's that we've created a culture that makes it unsafe for you to be vulnerable.

TARANA: Exactly! That's the rub right there.

BRENÉ: Yeah, it's not like you need less. It's just we've created a world where you're afforded less.

TARANA: Exactly. And this is why I feel like this book is so critical. Our humanity, our individual and collective vulnerability, needs and deserves some breathing room.

BRENÉ: That's beautiful!

TARANA: We need to live in an antiracist society, and people need to learn to be antiracist and practice antiracism. But I do not believe in your antiracist work if you have not engaged with Black humanity.

BRENÉ: Oh my God. Please say that again.

TARANA: I don't believe your antiracist work is complete or valid or useful if you haven't engaged with Black humanity. And so to that end, I feel like the audience for this book is first and foremost Black people, right?

BRENÉ: Absolutely.

TARANA: These pages are breathing room for our humanity. I learned so much about the Black experience reading these essays. It's not like Black people don't have anything to learn about the Black experience. Our experiences are vast and different. It's validating to see that even in our various identities and experiences, we engage in similar struggles, we have the same needs. And as other people engage with the book, it's about seeing the breadth of our humanity, and the depth of it, because this is the reality. It comes back to compassion and love. Always love.

BRENÉ: When I read the book as a whole, it was very, very overwhelming for me. Was it overwhelming for you?

TARANA: Yes.

BRENÉ: I mean, just as each essay came in—

TARANA: It takes your breath away.

BRENÉ: I kept thinking about bell hooks's concept of lovelessness and how she talks about lovelessness as the root of white supremacy and the patriarchy and all forms of oppression. And that the answer to lovelessness is love. I've read bell hooks for thirty years, but these essays and the process of co-creating with you taught me what love in the face of lovelessness really feels like. The marrow of it. When you say, "I don't trust any antiracism work that doesn't embrace and see our humanity," I can feel the call for love. I get it so fully right now. It's like you're telling us that if you don't see the heart and the love and the humanity and the joy of the Black experience—of Black humanity—then the antiracism work is bankrupt.

TARANA: Exactly. It's just like knowing something intellectually but not feeling it, and this is feeling work. It's heart work as much as it is head work. Those two things have to be in tandem. And I love that we have the ability to make this offering to Black folks who have felt stifled in this moment and overwhelmed and have not had space.

BRENÉ: Was your hope for the book, then, that it lands in the hands and hearts of Black folks who've had that experience that you've had, where you're like, *Oh my God. There's language for this. There's words for this. I'm not alone?*

TARANA: Absolutely. I haven't read many books about the Black experience that get past some of the first-layer stuff and really get into the heart work. And I just want us to see ourselves in this differently, to see our insides, the parts that we don't want to show people, the parts that we don't talk about often, the parts that we feel we have to cover and hide and keep away from the world in order to survive, in order to exist. I don't want to talk about my illness. I don't want to talk about my insecurities. I don't want to talk about how this thing really bothers me—but I need to and I can only do that with some semblance of safety. I want this book to be a soft place to land. "Give our humanity breathing room."

BRENÉ: I think you can make it that. I think we can. I think we can translate it because collecting and sharing these stories is breath and space and the act of seeing people. I don't know what to make of this, but every time I read an essay, I had this really paradoxical experience of a deeper understanding of how much more I have to learn about the Black experience, yet I saw myself and connected deeply to the shared humanity of the yearnings.

TARANA: That's so interesting, right? That's another reason why antiracist work is important. You have to engage with Black humanity, because the expansiveness of our humanity is so great that it reaches to other people. I don't want to sound all kumbaya and "we're all just human beings," but we're all just human beings whose experiences and environments and these systems have affected in different ways. But we must tear away the layers to reveal the core, then work our way back from that.

BRENÉ: One of the things that I learned a lot about is the unrelenting nature of intergenerational trauma.

TARANA: And that's not familial trauma. There are some things that have improved for Black people in the United States, and then there are other things that are exactly the same but with new faces. Systems that have not necessarily improved, they just look different. And we just keep trying to reshape the same tools that we use to dismantle the ever-changing systems. It's very tricky, but I do think this is a great moment for us to stop and focus on and give real attention to what effective dismantling looks like and requires. We need specific attention and action, not just general thoughts.

BRENÉ: I think I even feel different after this conversation, to be honest with you.

TARANA: Years ago, I went on a trip to Tunisia and it was for this big conference. It was a delegation of folks from the United States, from all over. I met this woman named Ra. She was a Vietnamese woman who also did work against sexual violence, also with young girls. We just connected quickly and became fast friends. And in the course of three or four days of us just talking, talking, talking, talking, I learned so much more about what Asian women, particularly the Vietnamese girls she worked with, have to deal with every day. There were very similar issues, very similar consequences, but very *different* reasons that explained how they had arrived at the places they were. I had the same experience with another girlfriend of mine, Thenmozhi Soundararajan, a Dalit Indian woman who does work around sexual violence among her people. We always landed in the same places. We often carry our trauma in similar ways, but the roads that led us to the trauma are all so different. We must pay attention to that road. That road is our humanity. That road is the piece that we're talking about. A lot of times, we're happy and relieved to find similarities: "Oh, you too? You too? Me too." No pun intended. These experiences create community, and it's wonderful, but it is still critical to understand the very different paths that led you to the trauma.

BRENÉ: That makes so much sense. We have to know the road if we're going to walk back down it and dismantle the systems that lead us to trauma.

TARANA: Exactly.

YOU ARE YOUR BEST THING

BETWEEN US: A RECKONING WITH MY MOTHER
—
JASON REYNOLDS

I WAS THIRTEEN WHEN MY GRANDFATHER'S LEG WAS amputated. Above the knee. An infection, they said. Something nasty spreading throughout his body. My mother and I traveled nine hours to South Carolina to ensure the oak tree of our family could sustain after losing a limb. I don't remember the ride to the hospital, or the hospital itself, but I do recall him sleeping flat-backed in bed, post-surgery, and my mother talking to the doctor (or maybe it was the nurse) about the dressing on the wound. A mound of gauze, as if the base of what was left of his leg, now footless and blunt, had been fashioned into a giant Q-tip. My grandfather had been turned into someone else. Someone I would never actually get to know, because he would never leave the hospital again.

I was thirteen when my grandfather's leg was amputated. Above the knee.

And thirteen when he died.

His death would mark the end not only of his life, or my mother's tangible relationship with her parents—my grandmother had passed three years prior—but also of our bimonthly journeys to the South. It had become routine for my mother to get off work every other Friday; have my older brother, Allen, and me pack the trunk with duffel bags and a small cooler containing a few aluminum-foiled turkey sandwiches; then give Allen a list of instructions of what not to do while we were gone, though she knew he wouldn't abide by a single word. But I suppose she figured his disobedience in absence was better than his persistent griping, which included tying each word to a disrespectful groan and taking everything in his life out on me by trying to take life out of me. Allen was afflicted with adolescence, and there was just too much ground to cover for my mother to deal with the futility of trying to cure him. Not to mention, at this point, my parents had come undone and she was doing this alone.

In the car, we'd listen to the radio—oldies—and I'd wait for my mother to ask the same question she asked every trip.

"How you know these words? You weren't even born when this came out," she'd say. Or, "Boy, what you know about the Temptations?" Or Marvin Gaye. Or Aretha Franklin. As if she hadn't been playing this music each day of my life. Their lyrics seemed to be spackled to the roof of my mouth, sharing space with the emcees of my time, an internal, intergenerational residence and resonance.

We'd pull into rest stops where I'd get peanut M&Ms, or gas stations where we'd load up on six-packs of peanut butter crackers my mother referred to as Nabs, to go with the turkey sandwiches, of course. Sometimes she'd even play a number. Out-of-town lottery felt luckier, she'd say. And whenever she'd get tired, whenever the hypnotic perforated line began to lull her to sleep, she'd crack the window and talk. My mother would sermonize about the importance of dreams and purpose-searching, meditation and energy. She'd say things about how she wanted me to live a grounded life, a centered life, and a life in flight all at the same time. Conversations she felt like she could have only with me—her child, a child—because the bulk of our family saw her crystals and smudging as the antithesis to their conservative views on God.

"Some things are meant to stay between us," she'd say.

My mother would tell me stories about growing up in a no-stoplight town on two hundred acres of land acquired by her great-great-grandfather, who was a freedman. How his chosen name after emancipation was January, and how no one actually knew how he got the land, but everyone believed he somehow inherited it from the family who formerly owned him. He built a house on this acreage, but he only knew of two types of homes—slave quarters and the big house. And to build slave quarters was out of the question. So he built a house resembling the one of the family who had treated him as property. And he tilled the soil and planted vegetables, grew fruit trees. Had hogs and chickens. He got married and raised children. One of those children, John Wesley, would inherit January's green thumb, making him the heir to the land. And as John Wesley grew older he would eventually informally adopt his grandson—my grandfather—whose mother had abandoned him for a life in the North. John Wesley raised my grandfather as his own. Taught him how to reap and sow. Taught him the value of hard work and heredity. Taught him family.

When John Wesley died, he left the land and the house in my grandfather's care. And that's where my mother was born and where she'd live until she was ten years old. It's where she learned to snap peas and pick cotton and pluck chickens. It's where she learned, as the middle child, how to take care of her older and younger sisters, the independent and dependable compass of a sometimes wayward sibling-hood. Where she, too, would learn family.

That land is the same land my mother and I would pull up to in the middle of the night, the darkness of Carolina a cataract to this country town. But the house wasn't the same house. It had burned down after my mother, aunts, and grandparents packed up and moved to Washington, D.C., for more opportunity in 1955. The farm had dried up, and the nation's capital—Chocolate City—was installing a new subway system and needed hands. So life in the country castle was traded for survival in a one-bedroom apartment in the projects.

Once my mother and her sisters were all grown and had children of their own, my grandparents moved back to South Carolina—back home—to their land. My grandfather built a new, smaller house with his hands, and used those same hands to wake up the dirt. Out came the collards, the mustards, the turnips and kale. Out came the watermelon. The cantaloupe. The tomatoes and butter beans. Before Allen was old enough to stay home by himself—and before the divorce—we'd come down every summer as a family, my father taking the wheel, Allen and me in the backseat ex-changing elbows. We'd had our first bouts with "everywhere-dust," and our first tastes of squirrel, buckshot still in the meat. We'd gotten to know our cousins, trained our ears to decipher their drawls, and, most important, were introduced to a part of our grandfather we'd never known. We'd only known a city man. But down South, we'd gotten to know a farmer. A giant who walked the rows, who sprinkled seeds and steered a tractor. A man who smashed melon on the ground and clawed the heart of it with his bare hands and passed it around to my brother and me like Communion host. There was a tenderness to him. A different kind of tenderness but a tenderness all the same. He wasn't one for hugs and kisses but was always sure to thank his children and grandchildren for coming to see him.

"I know y'all busy with your own lives, and you don't have to think about me and your mother down here," he'd say.

"You're my father," my mother would reply. "And you raised us to always put family first."

Then he'd pull a five-dollar bill from his wallet, press it into my palm as if it were a nugget of gold, and say, "Split that with your brother." And when I'd complain about how ridiculous that seemed, seeing as I'd surely blow half of my share on peanut M&Ms on the way home, he'd say, "Don't matter. Y'all brothers. Family."

I was seventeen when my mother was diagnosed with cancer. In her bladder. Caught it early enough, they said. It had eaten away at a part of her before she'd ever told me. But when she did, sitting across from each other at the kitchen table, I could see the bite marks. Could see the fear in her eyes.

"Don't worry," she said. "I'm gonna make it because I

need to see you make something of yourself. I ain't going nowhere until then."

So I was thrust into adulthood with a ferocity that seemed unfair and unforgiving. Struggling with college classes, working a boring but paid internship, then going to the hospital to check on my mother, who was in and out of surgery, chemotherapy, and radiation. I don't remember the daily ride to the hospital, and, honestly, I don't remember the hospital either. But I do remember seeing just her head lifted above the horizon line of white sheets. Her skin, ashen and cracked. Tubes. Beeping. And a spot of moisture always in the corners of her eyes. She'd squeeze my hand and nod just enough to let me know she knew I was there.

When I'd leave the hospital, I'd return to my hotbox of a dorm room, where I'd write for hours. Those lyrics I grew up listening to, the rappers and crooners, had somehow, through some backdoor miracle, transmuted into a love of poetry. So every moment I wasn't in class, at work, or in the hospital, I'd be scribbling well-intentioned self-righteousness to be recited aloud at open mics. It became both a thirst and a therapy, on one hand stretching a hole wider, and on the other smearing salve on a wound. I look back now and I wonder how much of it had to do with the weight of family complications, and how much of it was what my brother had—the affliction of adolescence, the natural irritation of growing up, let alone growing up Black. Either way, if it's true that you are what you do most, then over time the writing thing started to crystallize. It started to take hold. And as it did, my mother's cancer started to let go, easing its grip on her life.

I remember the doctor explaining to me the dressing on

my mother's wound. There were things in her that had been extracted. Parts of her no longer. She'd been turned into someone else. But she'd made it, which gave me the permission to leave.

I graduated, packed a trash bag with clothes, jumped in a U-Haul with my college roommate, also named Jason, and headed to New York City to chase my dream of being a writer. An unavoidable cliché. I'll spare you the details of the mattress on the floor and the forty-ounce beers for dinner. What's more important to note is that six months into my life in Brooklyn, I'd landed a literary agent, which at the time felt like hitting the numbers. Like my mother always said, sometimes out-of-town lottery feels luckier. But the thing about luck is . . .

I was twenty-two.

I was twenty-two when my mother was admitted to the hospital. Again. This time for vomiting and belly pain. Because of the previous surgeries necessary to remove the cancer, and the constant cutting into her abdomen, an immense amount of scar tissue had formed and had somehow wrapped itself around her small intestine, pinching it, blocking everything from passing through. To correct it meant risking her life. A twelve-hour surgery where any mistake could puncture the intestine and sepsis would bring on an infection she, according to the doctors, wouldn't survive.

I boarded a Greyhound at Port Authority and took the four-and-a-half-hour ride from New York City to D.C. to ensure the oak tree of this version of our family could sustain after losing bits of its bark. The trip seemed nothing like our rides down South when I was younger. No turkey sandwiches. No M&Ms. No Nabs. Headphones took the place of car speakers blaring Sam Cooke. And there was a man sitting next to me taking up more space than should be legal. More space than Allen ever did. Also, a baby was crying. Also, the bathroom had an encyclopedia of excrement strewn across its surfaces. Someone was sick.

There were no stories being told. So I told them to myself. Told myself tales about how I'd willed myself into this position. How I'd bootstrapped and hoofed from city to city, stage to stage, a troubled troubadour who'd taken the hard road and now it was finally paying off. See, while I was going to be with my mother the day before her surgery, I'd never planned to stay. The trip was going to be a down-and-back. A quick turnaround. Because the day of the surgery was also the day I was supposed to sign my first publishing contract. The day my dream was to come true.

I was twenty-two when I met myself.

I don't remember much about the night before. About getting off the bus or who picked me up from the station. I don't even remember how I got to the hospital the next morning. Maybe I rode with her. Maybe my mother was already there and I rode with my aunt. What I do remember is just after the doctors prepped my mother for surgery, just before wheeling her down to the operating room, I was able to stand at her bedside. Her face bare, the gold teardrop earrings she wore every day absent, as was the red lipstick.

"Ma, I want to be here, but today is the day I sign the deal. This is it. What I've been working for. Black boys don't get this kind of shot often. This is my purpose. My dream," I said, salivating at the thought of success. She nodded. Told me to do what I needed to do. I kissed her on her forehead, and was gone.

At twenty-two years old, I left my mother in a potentially fatal surgery so I could do what could've been done a day, a week, even a month later. But I thought about how I'd never seen Black writers growing up, so there couldn't have been many, and if I didn't do it then, they'd retract the opportunity and I'd never get to see who I might become.

Instead, I got to see who I already was.

I'm thirty-six now. My mother and I have never talked about the intricacies of that surgery, and whenever I ask about it, she brushes it off. But I know what happened. I know things got shaky, that there were moments when her life teetered. But she made it. Again. And today, as I write this, she turns seventy-five years old. This morning, before sitting at my computer, I called her. We talked about how proud we are of each other, and how our lives together have been nothing short of miraculous. I told her I was working on this essay, and about the shame I carried for over a decade. It sat heavy in me like a dumbbell in my belly, dragged behind me like laces too long. An infection. Something nasty spreading throughout my body.

"That was a long time ago," she said.

"I know, but sometimes I still feel it," I said.

"Baby, you gotta forgive yourself," she said, and went on to talk about how she raised me to go get what I desired. To go be who I wanted to be. To simultaneously live a grounded life, a centered life, and a life in flight. "But above all, I taught you like my daddy taught me—family first."

"Right. And that's the reason I—"

"And you've done that, every day since. Why be ashamed of what you've atoned for?" Once again, she was the independent dependable compass pointing true north. And in that moment, this moment, I realized that perhaps I've scratched at the emotional laceration of shame, of selfishness. But if my mother is right, the itching isn't coming from infection anymore, it's coming from the fact I've never removed the dressing from the wound.

"You understand what I'm saying to you, son?" she asked.

"I think so."

"Well, let me make it plain. Some things are meant to stay between us. But this ain't one of them." We talked for a few more minutes between tears and laughter, until finally I had to go.

"Happy birthday, Ma."

"Thank you, baby. And thank you for calling me. I know you busy with your own life and you don't have to think about me, so I'm always grateful when you do."

"Of course." I chuckled. "You're my mother."

THIS JOY I HAVE
—
AUSTIN CHANNING BROWN

OUR HORROR MOVIE COLLECTION CURRENTLY TOPS three hundred DVDs. They are divided into sections—zombies on the top, vampires in the middle, slashers on the bottom right. Hauntings line one side of the bookshelf, separated from the classics by a Freddy glove, Jason mask, and toy chain saw covered in fake blood. We attend conventions where my husband can get autographed pictures of his favorite horror stars. When October falls, we do not decorate with pumpkins and candles the color of burnt orange, but with gray skulls and tombstones. Every couple of days, when we admire the crisp air or changing leaves, one of us will playfully whisper in an ominous tone, "The harvest . . . is near."

It's silly. And though there are a handful of horror movies that I ban from entering our home because they feel a little too real, mostly I have come to appreciate the momentary terror of a good scary movie. There's a comfort in the relative familiarity of their beginnings: A delightful group of family members or friends is having the time of their lives.

There is laughter and joking, hugging and tenderness, an excitement for life hanging in the air. And then. And then there is a split second when the good time seems too good to be true. A certain grimness slices through the merriment. There is now only before and after.

It's a pattern that works because we intuitively recognize the jolt of fear that this is all too good to last.

Parents feel it when the kids are happy and relaxed and snuggling. Partners feel it when love swells and overwhelms. Students feel it when everything seems to be breaking their way. Pet owners feel it when the cute little face of their puppy or kitten is too much to bear. Entrepreneurs and creatives feel it after securing the big deal. In the moments when we are filled with joy, we wonder if there is a haunting force out there that will soon steal our joy away.

In her book *Daring Greatly,* our friend Brené calls this phenomenon "foreboding joy." She explains:

> We're afraid that the feeling of joy won't last, or that there won't be enough, or that the transition to disappointment (or whatever is in store for us next) will be too difficult. We've learned that giving in to joy is, at best, setting ourselves up for disappointment and, at worst, inviting disaster. And we struggle with the worthiness issue. Do we deserve joy, given our inadequacies and imperfections?

And so we find ourselves shrinking back from moments of joy. We recoil from the feeling, and to varying degrees from the *people* who bring us pleasure. We withhold excitement in exchange for the preparation of disappointment. We steel our hearts for tragedy rather than softening into the vulnerability that joy makes us feel.

I am certainly guilty of this. Whenever I talk with my only living grandmother (or even think about her for long), I worry that my joy means she will soon pass away. When my husband plans for me to have time to myself, I worry that he and my son will get into a car accident, all because I was excited to read a book without interruption. When I hug my father and breathe in the smell of his Grey Flannel cologne, I wonder if this will be the last time I feel his arms wrapped around me. It's a problem. And one I am working toward recognizing, in order to practice embracing joy rather than repelling away from it. I follow up thoughts of my grandmother with a text message to her, even if we just got off the phone. I breathe deeply and squeeze my husband and son before they leave. I look my daddy in the eyes and tell him how much I love him.

But I have discovered a far more despicable agent of foreboding joy in the form of racism. For Black people, and other people of color, there is a level of apprehension that isn't wrought from an uneasy feeling of undeservedness but from the knowledge that racism is the silent stalker always willing to wring joy from our lives. This level of foreboding joy is not in our heads; it's in the evidence of our experience.

As I type this, the world is in the midst of managing a global pandemic. It is common knowledge that in America, those who are elderly and Black are disproportionately more likely to die from illness—and so my worry is heightened for my grandmother. When my husband is in the car, I do not fear only the possibility of an accident, but the possibility of a police officer harassing him, maybe even taking his life. I'm all too aware that my father may not fall outside the statistics of Black men who have increased health problems compared with other demographics. For me, and many Black people, the data revealed by systemic racism isn't a vague notion but a real enemy that may turn and come after me, at the moment when I'm too joyful to pay attention.

Now that the weather is turning into fall here in the Midwest, my toddler has become obsessed with wearing a jacket. He will walk around the house pantsless but with a jacket fully zipped up, hands comfortably and confidently in his pockets. The other day we walked into the bathroom together. He placed his feet on his little plastic stepstool to reach the sink—and then pulled on the hood of his fleece jacket before turning on the water. As I glanced at his reflection in the mirror, he looked just like a tiny Trayvon Martin. For a moment I drifted into my head. *Did Sybrina Fulton look at Trayvon the way I am looking at you now, son? Did she have any idea her time with her boy would be so short? Will mine be? Will I lose you before you have a chance to become an adult? Will this racist country take you from me?*

I had to force myself to snap out of it, to stop rehearsing tragedy. I had to force myself back into the present moment. Because this kind of foreboding is not the result of undeservedness, but the result of knowing that I do not possess an antidote to the effects of racism. White superiority, which lashes out in racism, is wholly uninterested in deservedness. It is persistent beyond poverty, beyond socioeconomics, beyond educational attainment or even celebrity status. It does not care how hard you work or where you live. It is not interested in how you dress or speak. My skin means that I am always a worthy candidate to be the victim of white superiority and its tragic possibilities.

I am not alone. Recently I was a part of a book club in which other Black women in the circle began to ask questions about how to keep back this thief of joy.

A dark-skinned Black woman with long Senegalese twists wrapped in a bun atop her head said, "Austin, I have been unable to go for a walk since the death of Ahmaud Arbery. I love going on walks around my neighborhood, but I just can't bring myself to indulge."

An Afro-Latina mom leaned forward. "Austin, I'm going on an epic RV trip with my family, but I'm so scared about driving through the areas that have long been known as sundown towns. I'm having trouble really getting excited."

Another Black mother chimed in: "Austin, at this point I'm afraid every time my kids go to play outside. What if they venture into the wrong neighbor's yard or driveway? I know I can't keep them cooped up inside, but I also can't enjoy them playing freely outside."

As I listened to these women share about the specific ways their joy was being hampered by the ever-present reality of racism, I desperately wanted to assure them that everything would be fine. "Your walks are going to be sheer delight," I wanted to say. "You will encounter only kind travelers on your journey," I wanted to promise. "Your babies will be all right—no need to fear. Delight in their joy," I wanted to assure. But I couldn't. In good conscience I could not declare with any certainty that racism wouldn't continue to act as the villain in any good slasher movie. It might not be outrun.

What do you do when you are all too aware that Blackness makes you uniquely vulnerable in this world?

Traditionally, the Black community has relied on a spirituality born of hardship and humanity to declare a phrase popularized by gospel music artist Shirley Caesar, "This joy I have, the world didn't give it to me, and the world can't take it away." This is not to create a monolith of the Black community; I am in no way suggesting that all Black Americans have found refuge in the gospel of the Christian church. Instead, I mean only to point out a shared, rooted resilience in joy. Contained in this one sentence is a staunch declaration that if the world will take from me, it will do so only once, not twice. It cannot have both tragedy and my joy.

This posture is not giving in to foreboding joy. It does not suggest that since racism can steal from me, I will care about nothing and no one. Instead, it lives paradoxically at the intersection of joy and pain, realistically acknowledging that pain may come, but that pain cannot permanently drown out joy. After generations of horrific oppression, after a century of second-class citizenship, after a host of atrocities from colonization to genocide and all manner of horrors, we have learned that the only thing white supremacy would love more than taking our lives is for the lives we have to be diminished, less than human, filled with despair, containing only fear. But our community has learned that even the darkest depths of human evil cannot snuff out our experience of joy—of laughter and love, of good food and good conversation, of family legacy and hope for the future, of creative endeavor and the pursuit of justice. The joy of Blackness persists.

Our joy is in having loved and been loved well.

Our joy is in the ties that bind us to one another.

Our joy is in the legacy of all that our ancestors have done for us.

Our joy is in being able to participate in that legacy now.

Our joy is in the taste of freedom, regardless of whether we got only a morsel or the whole pie.

Our joy is in a shared language, a shared dance, a shared game, a shared song.

Our joy is in having left a mark in the world, being able to say, *I was here.*

And none of these things can be placed in a box and buried in the ground. They are resilient in that they are everlasting, surviving long after the pain of tragedy has waned.

There are very real ways our community attempts to keep the fear of tragedy away. A mother tells her son to pull his hood off before he enters the store. A partner reminds her wife to tuck the receipt away in case they are accused of stealing. Before leaving the house to walk the dog through the neighborhood, we double-check that we have ID to quickly end any accusations that we don't live in our own neighborhood. Even my husband and I, on our way to the hospital to deliver my son, sat in the car making plans between contractions. *If something goes awry with my labor and doctors do not believe me, we'll make clear that you are an attorney, and they should take us seriously. . . . No need to tell them your specialty is juvenile justice.* We do our best to anticipate the ways white superiority will pop up in our every day.

When the women in the book club asked me about the ways foreboding was inhibiting their lives, I asked them what parameters they could manage that might set their hearts at ease. *For a little while, can you walk at a public park, rather than in your neighborhood? Can you mark out your cross-country drive to stay in places as close to a major city as possible? Can you limit your kids to the backyard or the grass in your front yard, just for this week? Let's see if we can box the feeling in, knowing that we will not live at the pinnacle of anxiety forever.* Sometimes it works. Sometimes it doesn't. But we go on trying. We go on living, even if we are scared.

We decide not only that we will practice gratitude for the ways we are experiencing joy, but that we will do so with every bone in our body.

We will love hard.

We will dance with abandon.

We will laugh loudly and often.

We will declare our right to be in that store, or that school or that neighborhood or that job.

We will give our bodies the respect they so richly deserve for carrying us this far.

In the words of poet Toi Derricotte, "Joy is an act of resistance," and so we will lean in to that joy, knowing that our humanity demands that we fully partake of this magical experience.

When I look into my little boy's eyes and wonder if his life will mirror Trayvon's, I silently thank Trayvon Martin for his life and Sybrina Fulton for sharing his story. And I lean over to my little boy, kissing the top of his head. I let my heart swell with joy over his very existence in my life, for that little personality that is intrigued by zippers and pockets and hoods. I will love him harder, and in this become softer. I will be vulnerable—open to being hurt because I trust that my joy in him cannot be taken away.

DIRTY BUSINESS: THE MESSY AFFAIR OF REJECTING SHAME
—
TANYA DENISE FIELDS

I DON'T KNOW A TIME I HAVEN'T FELT GUILTY OR ashamed. This has colored literally every decision I have made in my life. And the more I let it lead, the more I fucked shit up for myself, the deeper the well of shame got.

I have felt ashamed of being dark, of having a broad nose, of my big lips, of my prematurely developed body, and later of my fat body with its rolls, saggy titties, hanging belly, and stretch marks. I have felt deep shame for not going to a better school, for not getting a good traditional job, for my struggles, for my literal hunger, for having six babies with four men who abandoned us. Sometimes, I was ashamed of being the one who stayed.

And all that shame ate me up, made me shrink, exhausted me, made me perpetually tired.

A few years ago I woke up, a 310-pound chain-smoker, with scratches around my neck, a bruised throat, and eyes almost swollen shut from crying all night. My kids' father had almost killed me. Our union had added two more children to my brood. We lived in a shitty-ass apartment on Fox

Street in a resilient and struggling part of the South Bronx. He was a ne'er-do-well "corner boy" who always fucked up his packs and came up short, and I was carrying the whole family. And even though I was his lover, surrogate mommy, and baby mama, he still had the wherewithal to become my abuser, emotionally, mentally, and physically, eventually almost killing me in front of my children after coming home from a two-year bid in New York state prison.

I had long become used to being a punching bag, or a doormat, or a real live masturbatory tool for the romantic partners in my life. And I had long internalized the ways in which people in my family and my community saw me.

Mammy.

That word had been thrown my way for most of my adult life, especially after the birth of my second child, and I was keenly aware that most folks were comfortable using it because of the way I looked.

My shame, my guilt for existing, for being viewed as ugly and undesirable, for surviving, has always been rooted in the way I look. It has not only lived in my body, it has been because of my body, and everything else has rippled out from there.

And sitting there in the 41st Precinct, being asked by some dismissive-ass white cop who couldn't be bothered to look me in my Black-ass face why it took me so long to disclose, I just felt the most tired I had ever felt in my fucking life.

What had shame gotten me? Shame doesn't course-correct or compel folks to make better choices. I was living in a community full of women who felt shamed, who had been born from shame, who projected nothing but shame. And it did nothing for us. It had done nothing for me. Shame is a liar, a thief, a murderer of dreams and vision. It is a manipulator. It, too, is an abuser.

I almost died in front of my kids and I was tired. Exhausted. Cracked wide the fuck open and broken into a million pieces by shame. And here I was just holding my guts in my hands and I got to see what I was made of. And it wasn't shame; it wasn't guilt; it wasn't ugliness, lack, or deficiency.

I am magic, cocoa powder, shards of glass and shrapnel, and the deepest parts of my grandmothers' imaginations. I am savory and sweet: salt, sugar, and lime, possessing the gentleness of the brightest lilies and the strength and temerity of the most destructive storms.

Most important, I am worthy. And that was the critical shift.

Language is important and words mean things. The things they mean can have an insidious effect on how we see the world, ourselves, each other. We use this word "deserving" a lot, and we think we're really saying something: "I deserve to be happy," "I deserve a nice apartment," or "I deserve a healthy and successful relationship," but deserving is transactional. It means you did a thing, performed a thing, earned a thing. It requires you to do something in order to get something. And for most of my life, shame robbed me because I thought I didn't deserve shit.

I had not performed respectability the way I was expected to. I made questionable decisions. I had "too many" children. I didn't earn enough money. I vacillated between working class and working poor, often needing the aid of safety net programs. And I lived in a world that told me from in utero that women like me don't "deserve" anything except heartache and pain because I was fat, because I was dark, because I was ugly by Western European standards, because I was "fast" and "let" older boys and grown men molest and rape me. This is the lens through which I saw myself, defined by others.

That became my narrative, and I wore that coat like it was the only one I had and every fucking day was freezing.

In this moment of deep exhaustion, of public humiliation, of desperation, of near-death spiritual disembowelment, I decided that to save my own life and not leave my children an inheritance of shame, poverty, and guilt, I needed to disavow this idea of deserving.

Joy, happiness, health, safety, love, and abundant community are inherent. You don't have to perform or do anything—for anyone—to get them. Imagine if we lived in a world in which this narrative was the one instilled in us instead of the capitalist, anti-Black one that roots us in lack, shame, guilt, and insecurity.

Right there in that chair, in that cold precinct, sitting next to this flushed, smug asshole of a cop, I decided to reclaim what was inherently mine. I didn't owe shame shit, but it owed me everything. I had finally bridged my political analysis with my real-life experience.

I had to contend with the reality that I had allowed shame to stifle any type of self-love and respect I should have had for myself. I had spent most of my life conceding that I was a trash can, only good for receiving the worst from folks. I felt physical pain finally confronting the hard truth that this was the example I set for my children and I asked myself, "If you can't love yourself enough to turn this around, do you love your children enough?" It was that love that propelled me forward on this journey; as cliché as it sounds, it was the love of my children and my desire to model for them what had not been adequately modeled for me that steeled my resolve to free myself.

That night, I had a family meeting with my six kids and we decided we were ready to leave, to go anywhere, but we would not suffer in this shitty apartment anymore. Through tears and silence and laughter we packed whatever we could carry, loaded up my fifteen-year-old Honda Odyssey, and drove to the PATH Homeless Assessment Shelter, a homeless intake center. And in front of another dismissive man, a Black one this time, I disclosed that I was a survivor of domestic violence. For two days we suffered in that place, and for four months we dealt with the abusive Department of Homeless Services. After leaving the PATH center and being assigned to a "transitional housing unit," I was subjected to curfews, to random folks letting themselves into our unit and checking our belongings, to roaches and mice, to fights in the building. It was awful, and quite often I asked myself what the fuck I had done.

I could feel that old frenemy shame sneaking up on me, whispering in my ear how disgusting I was, how I had made yet another poor decision, how I deserved everything I was getting. It took everything I had to push it down, to swallow it and then throw it up, to purge it. So, finally, after five years of suffering in this toxic and codependent relationship, I publicly disclosed on social media that I got my ass kicked on a regular basis, that I was often coerced into sex, that I was cheated on with impunity, that I was called names and put in harm's way, that my children had viewed some of this, and that I allowed this not only in this relationship but in others because I was nurtured in a world that instilled shame in me from the time I was birthed and probably well before. Before that disclosure, I had kept the inner workings of my private life a secret.

I was comfortable sharing—with thousands of followers on social media and hundreds of people I encountered during speaking engagements—very candid insight into my life as a mechanism for dismantling respectability politics, but up until this point I could never fathom sharing that I was a victim and survivor of intimate partner violence. I believed that in doing so I would seem weak, stupid, and fraudulent. Smart women, physically large women like me aren't victims, and on top of that it would seem like an admission to the very loud detractors that I was in fact a walking mess of a stereotype.

I finally, without apology, verbalized that I ain't felt like I was much of anything for a good long while and that it was not some personal failing but a natural result of a world laden with fat antagonism, colorism, toxic ideas around sexuality, respectability politics bullshit, and whopping doses of racism. And when all these things intersected, it made for a perfect low-self-image cocktail. I didn't "have" low self-esteem, as if it were something I had just picked up in the supermarket. This was inherited, this was nurtured, this was force-fed to me through passive words, casual slaps, and cyclical violence. It was normalized in media tropes and schoolyard taunts. It was insidious and invisible but always present and consistent. And the irony was that it was shame that created this, and it was shame that made me feel as if I could not openly verbalize and confront this and ultimately heal.

But fuck that, I said. Rebuke shame. So I said it loudly. I said it often. I was insistent, I was unrelenting. And then my sisters came out of the shadows, empowered and vulnerable, sharing narratives of violence, hurt, and the shame that was always right there, not really below the surface but subconsciously always moving the hand that led our lives. I was in turn empowered, and I found a powerful voice I didn't realize was there. I saw my reflection, what we were and what we could be. Suddenly I realized that happiness didn't have to be aspirational, that every good thing in this world that was denied to me and them because of some arbitrary bullshit ideology that we had no say in was inherently ours to claim, and I said that shit too. I said it loudly, sweetly, and abrasively. I was insistent, maybe even dogged, but I didn't care. I was giddy. This shit felt good, and I felt more free than I ever had in my life.

I didn't owe the world prettiness or femininity, softness or strength, desirability or thinness, timidity or boldness, children or chastity. The only one I owed anything was myself. I owed my children a happy and whole human to raise them. That would be my legacy for them, that would be their inheritance. I would start an endowment of radical joy and worthiness.

Through a newfound grounding in West African spirituality like Ifa from the Yoruba, family and individual therapy,

the exploration of radical Black feminist and womanist ideology, and an online and offline community of like-minded
Black women and femmes, I labored and rebirthed myself. I
kept my foot on the necks of those in DHS, making sure they
gave me what I needed. I was able to start to amass resources, including a contact on the mayor's Domestic Violence Task Force, to hold folks accountable. I was out of the
domestic violence shelter in four months. I found a bigger
apartment with room enough for all my babies, including a
giant master bedroom that I filled with artwork of dark-
skinned Black women and plants and pretty antique furni-
ture and a big, comfy bed.

I embraced joy as my birthright. Radical Black Joy is inherent as a human need and not some special trinket you
get after you rise high enough on the socioeconomic ladder
or unlock some special level of desirability or accomplish-
ment. I decided I would claim and manifest every fucking
thing someone told me I couldn't do—my birth mama, these
raggedy niggas who used my body as practice, my baby
daddies, the friends who kept me around to feel better about
themselves, and the overall society that inundates us from
birth with the message that certain folks are more deserving
and valuable based on their bodies, complexion, race, gender expression, physical and mental capabilities, educational levels, and whatever other fuck shit is just arbitrarily
made up and pushed into our minds and down our throats.

Claiming and manifesting these things goes beyond just
saying them. Rejecting shame is a messy and nasty affair.
Dirty business. It requires some serious shadow work to un-
hinge yourself from the manifestation of hundreds of years

of foolishness that shows up in every facet of your life. You commit yourself to being uncomfortable. I committed myself to being uncomfortable. You commit yourself to some of the worst emotional pain you have ever felt. I committed myself to that pain. You want to literally crawl out of your skin. It is not linear or exponential. And sometimes you realize that shame, hiding, shrinking, suffering is infinitely easier in the short term than the arduous and intentional work of getting spiritually and emotionally free. But you curate an abundant community that reminds you of what is on the other side, that loves on you, that pours into you, that holds you and sometimes shakes the shit out of you; you stay in therapy; you say the affirmations; you embrace it all because it's in the fire that you will be forged; it is there you will find peace and joy and liberation. It is in the fire that you destroy shame.

I have learned to let go of things that do not serve me. Shame does not serve me. Claiming what I have decided is mine does.

In the last two years, I have increased my overall health. I have hired six dope humans and tripled the budget of the Black Feminist Project, the organization that I have been working on tirelessly for the past ten years of my life. I give money to Black women and femmes, especially mothers, to do what they need to do with little to no scrutiny. I have made Mama Tanya's Kitchen, a lifestyle brand for boughetto Black women, a "thing," one that includes being hired to do short video content for one of my fave online brands, BuzzFeed's Tasty. I get hired to speak all over the country and sometimes internationally. I am actively working toward my goal of being a media personality. I have turned my home, in one of the roughest parts of the city, into a place of respite, joy, and productivity.

My children are beautiful and precocious. They are funny. They are happy and inquisitive. They are bold and defiant. They are having a childhood experience. We are stronger. And by sheer luck I have found love, maybe forever-love. It doesn't need to be, though, because for right now it is genuine, it is healthy, it is safe, it is happy, it is Black as fuck, it is intentional, and it is passionate.

My baby daddy, my most recent ex and abuser, was murdered a little while back. It was a punch to the gut when I found out. However, what was clear to me was that Tanya from two years ago would have been ashamed to lose a partner to gun and gang violence. It would have been one more indication that somehow I had made poor decisions in my life. My children's father was a "statistic," a "gangbanger" killed on New York City's mean streets, but in fact he was a full human being who at some point had hopes and dreams, who held deep trauma and pain. What could Wesley have been if he wasn't stuck in the muck and mire of shame, surrounded by a community of folks suffering from the manifestations of the same affliction? There was no shame, no embarrassment, just the complicated feelings of grief, sadness, and regrettable relief.

My story has become one of redemption but also of righteous indignation. I am indignant at the systems deeply rooted in anti-Blackness, capitalism, and oppression of anything seen as the "other" of whiteness that breed debilitating and invisible shame in women like me, in girls like the one I used to be. I am adamant and enthusiastic in my call to tear this shit down, to rip the fucking head off the beast that would stop my children from living fully actualized, free, and happy lives of abundance.

I don't want joy to be radical for Black women, femmes, and girls. I want it to be normal, to be expected, to be inherent.

I want us to fully be.

MY HEAD IS A PART OF MY BODY AND OTHER NOTES ON CRAZY

KIESE MAKEBA LAYMON

I DO NOT WANT TO BE KILLED BY A WHITE DOCTOR IN America. I think I will be killed by a white doctor in America.

That's crazy, right?

As a child, the word "crazy" bounced around every Black space I called home. "Crazy" was a destination and origin, pejorative and wholly emblematic of our abundance. I loved the word "crazy." I used it a lot in my oral communication with folks I loved and folks I despised. When we said "crazy" in my Mississippi village, it had either 1.5 syllables or 3.0 syllables. There was no way to actually spell the 1.5-syllable version. It wasn't at all "cray." It was more like "craze-a," if the hyphen was extremely faint and truncated, and the long "a" was sliced in half, where it almost looked like a sick "c" barely sticking out its tongue.

That's crazy.

The 3.0 version, reserved for extremely crazy shit, was "cuh-raze-ae," like when Grandmama and her husband, HaLester Myers, both went into diabetic comas after

Christmas dinner and white people—these young EMTs from Forest, Mississippi—first stepped foot in my grand-mother's house. The craziest part of it was how all of Grandmama's children and grandchildren—all laced with graduate degrees—started overenunciating words when those working-class young white folks came in the house.

We assumed that those white folks, the first to ever step foot in that house, had the power to save or kill my grand-mother and her husband. They were both extremely vulner-able, and our history with white folks, and our history with white folks in hospitals, let us know these white folks could eat our elders and their vulnerabilities if they wanted to without consequence. We hoped, not thought, our proper English would save them.

That's crazy.

I want to use the word "crazy" in more of my writing. Instead, I use the language of "health," "healing," "mental illness," and "reckoning." Rarely do I admit that I am indeed horrified of hospitals and terrified of white doctors. Some of this has to do with the fact that I've always been treated like a poor big Black man, even when I was a poor young Black boy, by white people. I've never had a tender medical experi-ence in my life. Instead of going to doctors, who I assume will treat me like a nigger, I've avoided them until the blood in my body hissed. While we Black men must embrace ten-derness and critically engage with our vulnerability, I also think it's crazy how often that vulnerability is gobbled up along with the rest of our bodies by the worst of white folks.

That's crazy.

I've spent every day of my middle-aged life avoiding

light, working and eating in bed, never eating in front of people, not answering the phone when family calls, not answering the door when friends come by, abstaining from that which brings me joy, expecting to die tomorrow, and hiding from people I know when I go out in public. This sounds crazy to me. When I was around people, at the strangest times, I'd get this fuzzy feeling in my head and heart, as if I were about to stop breathing. When a friend found me balled up on a wooden bench at work, they took me directly to the emergency room. The emergency room was packed, and I convinced my friend that I would call a doctor and make an appointment as soon as possible if they would let me go home and just lie down.

Three weeks later, when I had another experience of nearly passing out in my classroom, I went to the doctor. I used one of those strange James Baldwin/Nina Simone accents. I tucked my shirt in. I didn't wear sneakers. The doctor, a happy-go-lucky white man in his late thirties, checked my vitals. He checked my blood. He checked my heart. Initially, he said that they needed to send me to the emergency room because something on the tests "didn't look right." He ran the tests again.

"Oh, it's fine," he said. "We just need to schedule an appointment with a cardiologist to see why you keep feeling like you're going to faint."

I thought that was a win.

That's crazy.

I went to the cardiologist the next day. I greeted him as only Baldwin or Simone could. I wore the closest thing I had to penny loafers. I ironed my outfit for the first time in a decade. The doctor strapped a monitor to my chest to track my heart rate for the next week. At the end of the week, the doctor said there was a slight murmur but everything with my heart was fine. The following day, I kept feeling as though I was going to die. I kept avoiding people, kept swimming in the shame of professional, romantic, economic, and health failure. I googled "heart attack," "heart disease," and "chronic anxiety."

It took two minutes on Google for me to understand that I'd been having panic attacks. I couldn't understand why the doctors looked at my tucked-in shirts, heard my fake accent, and still refused to do anything other than treat me like a nigger.

That's crazy.

My problem, I guess, is that I don't think being crazy should stop us from being compassionate and actively regretful about structural or interpersonal harm we've caused. My friends who have been diagnosed as doctor-crazy say it's Black-crazy to think like this. I say that I don't think we've really considered whose doctor-crazy shields them from consequence and whose Black-crazy is fuel for disciplining and humiliation.

The only time I've been encouraged by a white doctor to tend to my mental health was when a white institution thought I was crazy for not wanting a school where I paid tuition to treat me like a nigger.

That's crazy.

When I was kicked out of Millsaps College twenty-five years ago for taking a book from the library without checking it out, I was absolutely crazy. The actions of the administration at my school and two of the fraternities were crazy-making. They, with help from all the whitenesses in that place, drove me crazy, or at least crazier. I asked those people, in my art and in bodily confrontations, to stop being so crazy-making. There is little in this world that is more revealing than asking grown white men to stop harming you and your people. Every time we ask or even demand that white folks stop harming us, we are saying, with all the vulnerability in the world, "You are hurting us like you've hurt my mama, my grandmama, my great-grandmama, and we'd really like you to stop."

"That's crazy," they always say, in a hundred different ways. "That's crazy."

Of all the terrifying things that happened the day I got kicked out of college, the most brutal was that I was told by the administration that I had a problem with white people, and that only a doctor sanctioned by the same administration who'd kicked me out of school could let me back in after a year. Vulnerably asking, and eventually telling, those white folks to please stop treating us like niggers was enough for me to get labeled as not just a threat, but a crazy Black boy whose mind needed tending to if I was to ever come back to school.

I so wanted to come back to that college after a year. That's crazy. But I was not going to let a white doctor paid by Millsaps College tell me that my desire to not be treated like a nigger in my city, at a school I paid to attend, was crazy.

That decision is still the most self-loving decision I have ever made, and that's crazy.

It wasn't until I talked with Dr. Imani Walker about a

project that had nothing to do with my crazy that I understood some of what was happening to my body, my head, and my relationship with "crazy" in college and today. Dr. Imani did more than give me the language of "depression" and "anxiety" and "chronic fatigue" and "disordered eating." She told me that everything I thought was wrong with me was everything the nation engineered to ail Black folk in this country. My first question to Dr. Imani was, "What's crazy?"

After my conversation with Dr. Imani, like a lot of my friends who regularly go to therapy, I started talking that *therapy talk*. I beat myself up for not believing my experience with Black doctors could be any different from my experience with white doctors. I used words like "sourcing" and "sublimate" in conversations that had little to do with misdirected sourcing or sublimation. That lasted a week.

That's crazy.

Part of my crazy compels me to imagine, and really obsess over, the radical possibilities of art. In the last few weeks of summer, though, that radical imagining necessitated commemorating radical realities I've yet to accept. I am a writer. I am a Black man. I am crazy. Actually, I am the child of two equally crazy kids from rural Mississippi. My crazy-ass mama lives alone on the East Coast. My crazy-ass father lives alone on the West Coast. My crazy ass lives alone in Mississippi.

That's crazy.

I have never seen my parents share a loving touch with each other or any partner, yet I know as young folks from rural Mississippi, they lovingly collaborated on my name.

Kiese was my father's best friend in the Congo, which is where he was when I was born. My father says his friend Kiese was crazy as hell. Mama was unconscious for thirty hours after they cut her belly open and pulled me out feet first. When Mama regained consciousness, she found that my father sent the names Kiese and Citoyen over to Grand-mama, who was with Mama every minute of labor.

Mama really wanted my middle name to be Makeba, after the South African singer Miriam Makeba. Now, a radical name does not a radical friendship make, but my name is Kiese Makeba Laymon because, at some point, no matter how short-lived, my crazy-ass mama and my crazy-ass father were invested enough in a crazy-ass radical friendship to collaborate on a name their child would spend a lifetime revising his crazy self into.

That's crazy.

A few months before the beginning of the pandemic, I finally went to the hip doctor. I was terrified. They took some X-rays of my hips first. As soon as I went into the doctor's room, I saw all these pictures of young Black men with big bodies like mine on the wall. The pictures were all of football players. The doctor seeing me was the doctor tasked with taking care of the football team in the area. When the doctor came in, I used that fake Baldwin/Simone accent while saying how incredible I thought it was that he did so much work with the football team. As I was talking, his nurse came in with the X-rays.

The doctor looked at them, then whispered something to the nurse. "How is it looking over there?" I asked as proper as I could.

The doctor said that on a scale of one to ten, with ten being the worst, my right hip was a nine. The left was a ten. I immediately slumped. Then I got invigorated because I knew I wasn't being "weak" when I complained about the pain. This was proof that my body was as fucked-up as I thought it was.

The doctor told me that if I chose to get a hip replacement, he'd be the one to do it. I told him again that my hips had been making life hard for nearly ten years. He explained how difficult the procedures are and suggested I might want to wait on surgery because I was so young. He asked me if I'd thought about getting shots in both hips that would make the pain go away for three months at a time.

"No," I told him. I'd never heard of those shots.

I knew this doctor did not want to perform surgery. I initially told myself it was because I was so fat. I wasn't going to let this man dissuade me from taking care of my body. "May we schedule the surgery, sir?"

That's crazy.

"If we do the surgery," he said, looking away from me, "the only thing is, I'm gonna have to do it."

That's crazy.

The doctor eventually shared something that let me know his right-wing leaning and gave me a scrip for Celebrex. I made the appointment for the shots in my hips. I got the Celebrex. I eventually went to the hospital in town and got shots in my hips. My pain went away for three weeks. When the pain really set back in, I was afraid to ask the doctor to refill my prescription. I didn't want him to help me. I didn't want him to hurt me.

That's crazy.

Over this pandemic, I've been doing something called "Ode and Apology." I started writing odes and apologies to folks I've disrespected and harmed. That was tough, brutal. But it was nowhere near as hard as writing odes and apologies to body parts I've mangled through neglect. So far, I've written to both hips, my eyelashes, the folds in my neck, my wrists, the right side of my groin, my molars, the mole on my left ass cheek, the base of my penis, and the backs of both thighs.

The hardest ode and apology was written to my head, my brain, because I seldom think of my head or my brain as part of my body. My head, too big to naturally come out of my mama, has helped me fly underneath the dirt of Mississippi. It's helped me float when my heart has been waterlogged. When my head has begged for help, I thought I was giving it help in the form of rigorous routines of writing and reading. Our relationship is asymmetrical. My head bails me out. I punish it for bailing me out. It punishes me for punishing it and I tell it to shut the fuck up because we're trying to work.

I actually don't know if I am doctor-crazy. But I know my head needs help. But my head needed help when I was in college. My head needs help now. I know that any love I purport to have for any human in this world is not nearly as radical or tender as it can be as long as I fail to give my head help. It's crazy what this nation does to our heads. It's crazier that many of us who have the means still think our heads are undeserving of help. I know our heads are worth risking humiliation so we can breathe. I know that continual humiliation in this nation leads to death. I do not want to be killed by a white doctor in America. I think I will be killed by a white doctor in America.

That's crazy.

If I write it one more time, I might actually believe it. That's crazy. Right?

THE WISDOM OF PROCESS
—
PRENTIS HEMPHILL

"Blackbird singing in the dead of night.
Take these broken wings and learn to fly.
All your life,
you were only waiting for this moment to arise."

—THE BEATLES

I AM A BLACK SOUTHERNER: TEXAS-BORN WITH Louisiana roots. I come from people who have survived some of the worst and don't make a practice of looking back. We have moved through always, with our culture, with our joy; and we were taught that you move through because you have to. It's what we've always done, sometimes even to the neglect of our healing.

Trauma, then, was also not what we called the things that happened between us, when the pressure and power-lessness exploded into intimate violence. Those were secrets and things we endured. We found hiding places in our bodies for all these memories, because no one I knew had the time or resources to heal. On Sundays, we took those places to church and prayed that we could be delivered from them somehow without naming them or feeling them or looking them squarely in the face. They were too big or too many or too close.

I grew up in a household that could as easily erupt in laughter and hugs and teasing as it could in violence. It's not easy to say this, even now. I know that my parents tried to love with the limited examples and the lingering trauma that they each had. As a child, you never knew which way the wind would blow, though. You knew that jobs were lost or never looked for, or that lights were turned off, or that checks bounced. But you never knew when those experiences, combined with a lifetime of pain, would come for you over a small thing. Growing up, we were told that our business had to stay in the family home. In Black families, this is not only a matter of decorum, it is a rule about safety—safety that is contingent on you being less yourself, and therefore, it is also about shame.

It is necessary for your safety that you know what this world finds dangerous about you. Brené Brown has defined shame as "the intensely painful feeling or experience of believing that we are flawed and therefore unworthy of love and belonging." It is "the fear that something we've done or failed to do . . . makes us unworthy of connection." This is the emotional weight that many of us carry. Shame is also the way that oppression becomes internalized. It is an emotional ritual for the marginalized. It is a practice necessary to maintain our already conditional belonging here. We feel shame about the aspects of ourselves that are most fundamental to who we are, that are tied not only to our actions but to our essence. Our Blackness, our genders, our Queerness, and all the things that accompany them—our skin tones, our shapes, our hair textures, our cadences, our desires. And we feel shame about the secrets we hold, many that we hold to keep us together.

For me, this meant that one of my first lessons was how to keep people a distance away. In some ways this was easy. My family decided to send me out of my community to a school that was predominantly white, across town. It was one of the most profound shapings for me around shame as a requirement of belonging. It was a lesson in pretending— pretending that I knew the New Kids on the Block songs they sang, when I listened to New Edition. Pretending that I lived near them and shopped at the same stores. Pretending that the comments and the names didn't hurt when they did. Pretending that my home was a steady place. Growing up, I only ever invited one friend over to spend the night. She was one of the four other Black children in my fifth-grade class, but unlike me, her family had enough money to live where white people did. Their lawn was always mowed and their house did not have roaches. The Saturday she was supposed to come over, I spent the morning killing every roach I could find, thinking it was possible to kill enough to be accepted. When she arrived, I planned to walk into every room loudly, offering any surviving roaches the time to scatter. When she came, I showed her around the house, doing my best impersonation of a real kid who was not ashamed or afraid. As soon as I turned the light on in my room, a roach, on cue, casually flew across the room. It sank me. I launched into a story about the differences between water bugs and cockroaches before letting shame and silence swallow me. She never said anything about it, then or later, but I remember lying awake that night with tears, biting my lip to stay quiet. *This is why you don't let people over, this is why you don't let them in.*

When I got to be a teenager, my sexuality and gender expression refused to iron out into something more respectable. The tomboyishness that my grandmother identified in me only matured into a Queerness that refused binaries and easy categorization. My sense of belonging became even more unstable. For months, I prayed at night that I would wake up changed, interested in different things, with different desires. When I kept waking up as myself, I started praying that I wouldn't wake up at all. When my family finally "found out" I was Queer, it was devastating. It wasn't that they hadn't suspected. It was that in being told, they felt that I had chosen my identity over them. I had forced them to carry shame for my unruliness. And in their rejection of me I could sense all the things about themselves they believed had to be hidden or compromised in order to belong, and the expectation that I could or would do the same. To insist that belonging shape around me and receive me as I am was a paradigm shift that seemed too dangerous for a world where all of our belonging was tenuous. So for a period I was expelled. I left home, moved across the country where there was less contact and what felt like less love. I took with me a mountain of shame that would sometimes become defiance but was always at its root a longing to return.

As an adult, the shame I experienced around the traumas of poverty and abuse made it almost impossible to allow and maintain intimacy. Always lurking was the fear that I would be found out, that if I invited someone over and turned the lights on, something would fly out, namely who I really was. I hadn't, though I longed to, experienced the sense that I could belong as I am, with my story and with my experience.

IT'S IMPORTANT TO NAME that this task of healing sits against a political backdrop, and that backdrop doesn't allow us to simply individualize healing or imagine that it could ever be an apolitical endeavor. For Black people, many of the tools and technologies used by our ancestors to heal have been taken or suppressed. And the extent of the traumas we have experienced has been constant and collective, overwhelming our efforts and our resources to address.

In many ways, the moment in which we find ourselves is calling for each and all of us to acknowledge and address the existence of Black pain and trauma, finally and with consequence. Each death and each riot activates another memory of another life lost without justice or reason; this is how trauma unhealed haunts and accumulates, reemerging and reanimating the body. It does not disappear. The study of trauma has been itself a way to name human pain that lingers and lives on after rupture, especially in the individual, but increasingly also in the collective. We understand more now about how trauma winds and warps, inhabiting bodies, permeating relationships, and shaping lineages. This country has made a practice of denying the existence of trauma in Black bodies and communities and also denying its own role, ultimately, in traumatizing us. We've also denied and ignored it; our pain has not been a consideration that many of us can afford to feel. So we cope and adapt and make private rituals to honor who has been lost and what of us is lost in their leaving.

Denial, though, is always a temporary fix. Each experience is still waiting to be felt, honored, and understood— waiting is the undeniable impulse the body has toward healing. Healing this generational trauma requires an end to what continues to traumatize us: police violence, the violence of generational and systemic poverty. It also requires our commitment to the feeling, to the ritual, to the process that will make us anew. On the other side of healing is not a return to what has been, but instead renewed purpose, deeper relationships, and dignity for the collective.

Like many others, I came to political work with an unspoken and unconscious motivation to create and experience belonging. I had trained as a therapist and somatics practitioner and spent some years counseling in my community before I came into Black Lives Matter Global Network as the Healing Justice director and then later as a politicized somatics teacher. In everything I've done I've wanted to create spaces where poor people, Queer and trans people, Black and Brown people, and formerly incarcerated people could heal without being retraumatized in the process. I had been in too many therapeutic rooms myself that were unsafe, where I had to keep things hidden so as not to be pathologized or blamed, in the way that it is our habit to blame bodies like mine. I wanted a space, however small, for my community to look across the room and not have to hide. I'd been working to create a world that would know how to embrace a child like me, one that would make room for my family to heal. It hasn't always been as clear to me how personal it was, how much of my work was a working-through of my own pain. But healing our lineages is also healing our lives.

That we parse healing and politics apart is some of what plagues us. To understand uprisings or to understand protest, you have to understand emotional repression. You have to understand that there are feelings that we have not allowed. Rage forms when grief has not been allowed or honored. What I have experienced in the streets is the convergence and expression of grief that spans generations, grief that has been silenced and unacknowledged but lives on in us. This is also for so many of us the practice of healing shame, of moving beyond the frame of respectability that we have been told keeps us safe but doesn't.

What are our politics if not the method through which we create and distribute wellness with what we have? What is culture if not our practices of resilience?

I STARTED MY HEALING journey in my mid-twenties. I'm not sure how I found my way there. I hadn't known anyone who had even done therapy outside of forced institutionalization. But I knew that I couldn't sort out alone the things that I was trying to sort out. I needed to feel that I could be upset by my family, be hurt. I needed to honor the truth of what I experienced while processing the magnitude of the systemic impact of trauma on my family, how long and for how many years things had tried to break us apart. The force of history landed on my family—on each of us—in our relationships, and the constant nature of it didn't leave room for healing.

I remember working years ago with a somatics practitioner, addressing the stories and traumas that live in my body. We had found a contraction, a place in my chest that was almost constantly seized up, protecting me, I discovered, from revealing myself. I came up against the fear that I wouldn't know myself if I let this tension go. I wasn't sure I would trust the person who would come tumbling out; and I wasn't sure, most of all, that I could ensure their belonging. Being myself had for so long seemed a dangerous thing. As soon as I felt it, something in me knew that the contraction ultimately wasn't me. I was the person who was there before the oppression, before the trauma, and before the shame tried to dictate who I am.

Healing brought me into a face-to-face confrontation with belonging, with the strategies I had developed to hide, the stories I told about not needing anyone that made the hiding easier. Healing had me admit that it was closeness I wanted, love and relationship and family who didn't ask me to hide.

Healing trauma in individuals has never been an easy task. In doing it, we are in fact moving to the body's edge and through the waves of memory and impulses designed to protect our lives. We are revisiting the compromises the body has made to safety, belonging, or dignity in order to survive. And we are finding another path internally where these can be restored, bringing us back into connection, feeling, and community.

Black trauma is a concentration of generations of these experiences, experiences that overwhelm not only the individual but the community, enforced and enacted through policies that have displaced us and criminalized our cultural practices that help us heal. It is also the trauma of systematic denial of resources or stability needed to address the pain and aftershocks of massive collective trauma and daily assaults and indignities.

We have survived through a persistent commitment to life, by filling simple lives with big love and a commitment to justice. And the truth of the matter is that the need for healing does not disappear because we have found a way to survive. This work of healing waits for us in moments of stillness or intimacy, in the persistence of doubt or shame, in our struggles to find or sustain stories of meaning or risk living into our purpose. The dissonances we can feel are all the breaks we survived, waiting to be unraveled through feeling, waiting ultimately to free us and our lineage.

Our pain aversion makes this question of healing challenging to approach. It is one of the central motivators in American culture, to win our way to a pain-free existence. This does not mean that we do not experience pain—all of us do—but it means that we hide it, we deny it, and we transfer it as custom. It means that we shape the world to outsource suffering, that we create structures to concentrate this pain and mythologies of superiority to justify it. These are the mechanics of oppression. It is the organization and distribution of trauma across a society. Those with more power can choose more of their pain.

But pain serves a role in a life. When experienced at a

digestible rate, when our belonging and safety are not at risk, it can develop us. It can sturdy our sense of ourselves and open up the capacity for empathy. It can remind us that much of what there is to feel can be felt, in our bodies or with support from our relations. And yet, pain disproportionately felt, without space for respite or relief, without accountability or acknowledgment, creates a thing that festers.

Healing Black trauma is one of the most worthwhile endeavors we all can undertake. It is one that calls for the remaking of all social relations and an examination of our structures and the principles on which they are built. How has denying Black pain narrowed all of our lives? Where have we gone numb to our trauma, imagining that it is too big to face?

My work of healing is about recovering Black life span, which is whittled away by the body's constant stress. This is the work of recovering Black possibility, creativity, and futures. This can happen in individual healing and therapy; that is some of how I've come to face my own secrets. It is also the work of something bigger: culture, ritual, spaces we create together, our commitment to caring for each and all of us.

We can imagine that the purpose of healing is to restore Black people to a mythic past or propel us into a whitewashed version of the future. I don't think healing follows directions. The truth is that I don't know what we become when we heal. None of us does. That is the wisdom of the process. I know that when I opened up to myself I became more of me, I became curious and porous. I cried more and argued less. I knew where my fight belonged and where it didn't. I knew where I belonged and I insisted on remaining. In healing we become more of ourselves. We move away from controlling our expressions, insisting on who we will be, gatekeeping to manage our insecurities, and we discover who we are after all this time, after all these breaks, with all this joy. I am proposing a process, not a destination. A necessary process for us to become, a process that will fundamentally reshape us and our relationships, and will have to, by its very magnitude, reshape the world.

LOVE LIFTED ME: SUBVERTING SHAME NARRATIVES AND LEGITIMIZING VULNERABILITY AS A MECHANISM FOR HEALING WOMEN IN THE BLACK CHURCH

—

TRACEY MICHAE'L LEWIS-GIGGETTS

THE WOMEN WERE BEAUTIFUL. THEIR EYES, TINTED the whitish-blue of burgeoning cataracts, were simultaneously dark and mysterious, hinting at stories they'd never actually tell. Their rich, smooth brown skin belied their seven, eight, or nine decades of living. I remember watching them with the kind of curiosity only a child could have. I wanted to know the motivation for their clasping of hands in worship or raising them high in praise. Why did an avalanche of tears escape down the sides of their cheeks? Why did their mouths move in silent prayers? And when sound finally found air, why was the melody released into the atmosphere heavy with longing, a longing I now identify as unattainable liberty?

"Love lifted meeeeee. Love lifted meeee.

When nothing else could help, looooove lifted meeee."

The elder women of the Black Baptist and Pentecostal churches I grew up in, as in most Black churches, were too often the secret keepers. They knew where the bodies were buried. But by being vaults, they often unwittingly became the arbiters of shame. They invested in a theology rooted in patriarchy from the pulpit. They wielded their power as elders to ensure that younger women toed the line of Christian decency.

These same women would throw scarves over the legs of women and girls in skirts deemed too short.

"Don't go tempting the men, child!"

"Don't be one of those fast girls."

These same women would loud-whisper about the single mother with four babies and her lack of self-control. Or the young girl who talked too much, who was too "smart for her own good." All this, despite the fact that many of them never spent a Saturday night in a cold bed, and as far as being too smart or talking too much, they practically ran the church as well as any corporation.

This duality seems to suggest that the shame divvied out by these "mothers" was never about any particular act but the exposure of those acts.

"Never let the right hand know what the left hand is doing, baby."

They bought into the narrative that women should appear silent and submissive despite their actual reality of being very vocal and less than deferential. They too often tried to harness the audacity of women and girls who resisted those lies.

"Men are the head, but we are the neck, and we turn the head any way we want without it realizing it's being turned."

For these Black churchwomen, standing bold in their truth and being freely vulnerable was the purview of rich white women, who had the privilege of both fearlessness and tears.

In addition to the tamping down of our intelligence and sexuality, these women were not supposed to cry about any of it. To deal, we were only supposed to sneak sips of cognac from the flasks held in our bosoms. Or maybe take an extra one of those white pills with the number ten on the back. Or stuff our faces with that three-piece dark chicken on white bread with extra hot sauce. We were supposed to do whatever it took to silence that part of ourselves that wanted both Jesus and liberty. There was no room for mourning the station in life we'd accepted. Any emotional expression of our pain was a sign of weakness or rebellion. So we saved our tears for high worship because, at least then, we knew God could bottle them up.

This contradiction—dare I say, hypocrisy—reveals how shame has infiltrated the Black church but still doesn't account for the reality of the Black experience as an intersection. It's unreasonable to explore a larger conversation about what it means to deal with shame in a religious, and specifically Christian, context without unpacking the intersecting influence of race and gender issues.

GROWING UP A
BLACK CHURCH GIRL

Many Black girls who grew up in the church learned how to perform our worthiness early on. We watched the mothers of the church in the basement kitchen putting together after-service chicken dinners and basking in all the praise for their mac and cheese. We watched Sister So-and-So sing the walls down and get the immediate gratification of people passing out in the aisles and crying out to God in a kind of orgasmic exaltation all because she "let the Lord use her." I learned that knowing all the answers in Sunday school Bible trivia garnered me "That Tracey is so smart" or "Oh, she's gonna be somebody someday." Those words were my salvation, probably more so than Jesus was, if I'm honest. And by themselves, the words weren't the problem. We should praise our children and reward them for good deeds and behavior. But the unintended consequence, what lay just underneath the words, was the things never said when I was quiet and truly being myself.

What does one do when the shame is wrapped in love? When telling a girl to "keep quiet" because "that's just the way these men are" is a mode of survival because little Black girls who are hurt and in pain just aren't as valued in this world as little white girls? There is a thread of protection that lines the shame of those church mothers, a protection of themselves and their own minds so they don't have to waste time they don't have reconciling their whole belief systems. Protection for their baby girls, who will likely enter a world not that much different from the one they've known.

The church has created a space where Black women have been able to adapt to our diminishment in a way that feels like there is some reward on the back end for doing so. The more we suffer, the more "crowns in heaven" and whatnot. And the sad part is, some of us have so internalized such a skewed and distorted version of our faith tradition that we perpetuate this kind of emotional and spiritual violence on other women. To the point where men no longer have to be the enactors.

THESE NOTIONS OF NOT being entitled to protection are real for Black women. Such was the reality for enslaved African women and to some extent it is still a reality for Black women today. Missing from so much of the scholarship on shame is how the reality of systemic oppression affects a Black woman's ability to be safely vulnerable on a much larger scale than just our personal relationships. We can believe in our inherent worth and value all we want, but moving through a world where our very survival often depends on an acceptance of dehumanization makes healing from trauma complicated. We are swimming in a cesspool of shame, breathing in our own contempt—to the extent that many of us believe that the only way to truly live is to grow steely-hearted gills and adapt.

My particular story is, sadly, one of millions. A Black girl child molested in the dawn of her adolescence. Sent away to "keep the family together." Immersed in a faith tradition that held no space, no room for my story and thrived on the silence and complicity of its members. Confusion settling in my soul and driving every relationship I'd ever have for the next forty years, I would inevitably find myself entering middle age, desperately battling the war of anxiety and PTSD that had freely waged against my mind and body for nearly all of my life. Determined to climb out of the muck of a shame narrative that should have never been mine, in order to heal. Realizing that deconstructing my faith was the only way to do that and maintain any semblance of spirituality. Doing that healing work required therapy, and it was in therapy—EMDR, specifically—where I encountered a visceral response to ambiguity. I was more than a control freak. The need for certainty had defined every area of my life and hindered my ability to move forward in areas that appeared too "gray" for my liking.

SHAME AND CERTAINTY

Church folks' unwillingness to surrender our certitude often becomes a driver for the shaming that happens in the church. We have to be right. About the tenets of our faith. About the way God shows up. About the rules and regulations we wield to keep the "flock" in line. Because what does it mean to not know for sure? Can we still believe if we lean into the mystery of God and accept that maybe there is more than one answer, more than one interpretation, more than one way to embrace faith?

Jesus did not shame or shun the woman with the alabaster box who believed she needed to wash his feet with her tears and hair in front of a community of mostly men who tried to debase and degrade her (see: Luke 7). Jesus did not shame the Samaritan woman who was living with a man she hadn't quite yet made husband number six (see: John 4). He called out her truth, yes, in the midst of a dialogue with her—something that happens often on our spiritual journeys—but there's no indication that he made her feel unworthy in His presence despite the fact that the cultural context said neither a man nor a rabbi should be seen speaking to a woman, much less a Samaritan.

A long way from the teaching of Jesus, the Christian church too often uses shame as a tool for control and manipulation, but even when we think it's working, it's not. In fact, what's actually happening is that folks who have been shamed by the church have become disenchanted with the faith; what should be safe and holy communities only look like rigid and loveless institutions. American evangelical churches, in particular, cling to law and government as tightly as their interpretations of the Bible, but don't seem to realize that the Jesus they claim as Savior would have likely broken those laws in order to extend love, peace, and wholeness to those identified as the "least of these" (the marginalized). That kind of restoration lives at the core of the salvific work of Christ.

But we miss all that and, in turn, miss the opportunity to be agents of the Spirit's healing—because we are too deeply invested in certainty as a marker of our faith. Ironic since, by definition, faith requires a relinquishing of certainty.

I'm not sure that we can avoid personal experience shaping how we think about God. If we believe that historical and cultural context matter, then it makes sense that those events don't happen in a vacuum. They happen to people and show up as personal experiences. And it's very important, even good, as long as we are conscious that it is our personal experiences shaping our theology. As long as we are not calling that influence absolute truth.

My experience as a little Brown girl growing up in the church in Kentucky very much informs my perspective of God—even when I wish it didn't. But the critical piece here is that I'm aware that it does. And that awareness means I can check myself when I make certain assumptions about people that are rooted in my experience and not necessarily in anything God has done or is doing. Beliefs aren't ever objective, and I don't think they need to be. I don't think we should want them to be. Thinking in such rigid and stagnant ways keeps you locked into this desperate need for certainty. And if you are so certain about everything, then even God won't be able to tell you any different about what you "believe." Your certainty becomes an idol in the face of a God who never changes but is ever moving.

The need to feel certain in our faith derives from a real and honest place for Black folks. The church promises certainty with its proclamations and rules. The perceived upside to these certainties includes having clear markers for how to live in a world that has different rules for Black people. For instance, an emphasis on not having premarital sex, as problematic as that is, might prevent a single motherhood that is shunned by the larger society when those mothers are Black. If children and teens are forced to attend church three times a week, then those are three days parents don't have to wonder what's going on with their children out there.

But the downside, the part of this alleged certainty that does the most harm to Black women, is that it has a tendency to wield shame as a mechanism for keeping us in those boxes—even when we choose not to be. We find our safety there, and anything that disrupts that box is ousted like a demon or called one directly. The shift that needs to happen is one that aligns with the gospel the most. Embracing mystery leaves room for our own mysterious emotional responses and allows love to fill us up in ways that our certain faith never could. As Brené Brown wrote in her book *The Gifts of Imperfection,* "Faith is a place of mystery, where we find the courage to believe in what we cannot see and the strength to let go of our fear of uncertainty."

This is why the language of certainty—binaries like *do this and go to hell, don't do that and go to heaven*—are so problematic. Not a single major figure in the Bible took the straight-and-narrow path. Most took the long, arduous way because, from God's perspective, that was the best route for building the character and confidence necessary to sustain the destiny. That said, I do not think God is terribly interested in blocking or stealing our human agency. Only humans do that to other humans. And Black women in the church have been regular recipients of such thievery.

A MISGUIDED THEOLOGY
OF SUFFERING

The shame narratives that define too many of our experiences haven't come out of nowhere. They are deeply rooted in a Westernized, white-supremacy-laced theology unknowingly embraced by the Black church. In addition, patriarchy has been so threaded in our interpretations of Scripture that the glorious liberation that Jesus offered all of us, and women especially, is buried under the religious infrastructures many men need to exist in order to maintain a power they perceive as their divine right. Melissa Harris-Perry nails this point in her book *Sister Citizen: Shame, Stereotypes, and Black Women in America:*

> The disobedience of Eve in the Genesis story has been used to justify women's inequality and suffering in many Christian traditions. Thus, what is understood as women's complicity with evil leads much traditional theological reflection on suffering to offer the "consequent admonition to 'grin and bear it' because such is the deserved place of women." Similarly, when Jesus is seen as a divine co-sufferer, the potentially liberating narratives of Jesus as a revolutionary leader who takes the side of the poor and dispossessed can be ignored in favor of religious beliefs more interested in Jesus as a stoic victim. Christ's suffering is inverted and used to justify women's continued suffering in systems of injustice by framing it as redemptive.

The glorification of suffering in the faith generally provides credence for the suffering that Black folks face in the world as a result of oppression. We grab on to the former because it helps the latter all make sense. And yet, the bulk of that suffering falls on the women, who really are the engines of any Black church, from Birmingham to Chicago, Philly to Oakland. Racism drives us toward the suffering narrative, and patriarchy sustains its negative impact on women. As a result, too many of us choose the theology of "we must suffer" versus "we will suffer." While *will* speaks to inevitability—a global, human truth—the *must* implies that there is something inherent in us that makes us easy collateral damage for the male ego.

LOVE WILL LIFT US

But there are some of us who want more and who believe our Creator wants more for us. We are not going to swim in the crap or contort and disfigure ourselves in order to adapt to a world that doesn't see our *Imago Dei*. We are jumping out of the bowl and into our freedom, as frightening and uncertain as that space above feels.

When I think about potential solutions, ways to subvert the shame narratives, I can't help but return to those hymn-singing elders of my youth. The typical perspective on transgenerational healing is that future generations must heal in the stead of our mothers and grandmothers. I agree with this and have watched it play out over and over again. But I also think we'll see a real shift when Nana feels like she can get free first. I'm reminded of my mother who constantly says, "I'm too old for therapy" or "That stuff is for y'all young folks." What if she knew that it was never too late to release the shame that's held her hostage for all these years? A free Nana means all of us can heal no matter what or when. When Nana gets free, then Mama and Baby Girl can access freedom at any time also. Nana's liberation might create a model for safety and not just survival.

What does this look like in the church context? Well, instead of a stern "Cover yourself!" Nana gets to chuckle or laugh with that young woman in the short dress about the time she spilled ketchup on her yellow micro-mini in the 1970s. In their laughter and in her acceptance, intimacy forms and a relationship takes root. That kind of nurturing love, as opposed to the transactional way we often experience love, is absolutely a way to counter shame in the Black church. The healing that comes from it is also a kind of resistance against the narratives that try to diminish Black women elsewhere.

God doesn't define us by our worst moments. God *does* hold us accountable for repeated bad moments. We can't use God's grace to justify oppression and injustice. We can't use the grace of God to excuse any violation of another's humanity. This is true whether we are talking about the unarmed Black man killed by police or the young woman pummeled by shame because the church doesn't take the time to nurture her heart.

I often wonder who I would have been if I hadn't had the fire molested out of me as a child. If I'd felt that my voice and my questions would have been embraced in the churches of my childhood. If I'd been given tools for healing that extended beyond Scripture memorization and silence. There's no way to know. What I am clear about is this: One day, when I'm old and gray, with whitish-blue rings around my failing eyes, and I find myself belting out my favorite hymn: "Love lifted meee. Loooove lifted meee. When nothing else can help, looove lifted me," I won't have to only reach up for my peace, but I will be able to reach out into a faith community that values my mental, emotional, and physical safety over just my survival.

Love absolutely will lift us. But there are generations of Nanas, Mamas, and Baby Girls looking for something else to help. The church has so much more than shame to give us.

NEVER TOO MUCH
—
MARC LAMONT HILL

I WAS ABOUT FIVE YEARS OLD WHEN IT HAPPENED. I don't recall who it was, but somebody in my family said something that hurt my feelings. I don't remember what they said. And I don't know if it was even particularly hurtful. But I do remember crying. I cried a lot when I was a boy. Too much, I was told.

I was different, I was told. I was "too sensitive," an observation that felt like both a judgment and a reprimand. Too sensitive. These were words that carried suspicion and wariness. Too sensitive. These words are among my earliest memories. They have haunted me ever since.

As a young child, I was quiet. Like my mother, I was a reader. I didn't want to run around outside as much as my brothers, and I had not yet been bitten by the basketball bug that hit most of my neighborhood. Instead, I wanted to stay in the house or sit on the steps, losing myself in the books my mother brought home from work. These were not, I would learn, suitable choices for a Black boy, particularly one growing up in North Philadelphia.

This isn't one of those gently anti-Black stories about anti-intellectualism or homophobia in my community. As Americans, we were as susceptible as anyone else to those elements. But not exceptionally so. We were human, not pathological. Something else was happening.

I was loved. Deeply. But we lived in a world framed by suffocating ideas about who a person—who a Black person, who a Black man—needed to be in order to be safe and happy. This world held few safe spaces for little Black boys who moved through the world in the ways I was naturally inclined to move. So I learned to move differently. I learned not to cry.

I learned that my humanity was bound up in my masculinity. I was taught that my masculinity was best shown through physical strength and paying bills and controlling space and being emotionally lean.

And although we don't want to admit it, there was a functionality to this type of masculinity. As unhealthy as our performances were, looking tough and acting "hard" meant that people would be less likely to test us. Looking like we could fight meant that we wouldn't have to fight. And most of the time, deep down, we didn't want to fight.

We just wanted to live. We just wanted to be loved well. We wanted to be seen. We wanted to be respected. We wanted to be human.

My model for manhood came from my father. He held our family close and led us through storms, including the ones created by his own unhealthy masculinity. Although he was an educated man, he loved to work with his hands. He spent most of his free time fixing the broken-down rental properties he owned. The repairs, the painting, the roofing, he did it all himself. I would run behind him on the way to whatever property he was fixing. He would call out from the front of the car, "Put that book down. Look at that building they're putting up over there!" Part of that was, I'm sure, teaching me to be more social and observant. The other part, I think, was about balancing me out, pulling me away from the boy who sat on stoops and read Judy Blume while other children ran around.

Like most men of his generation, my father showed little emotion and no vulnerability. And what other examples were there? Pop culture gave us *The Cosby Show,* but the Huxtable world of expensive art and famous friends was too foreign to seem real. And the other shows—*Diff'rent Strokes, What's Happening!!*—didn't have present Black fathers. *Good Times* gave us James Evans, Sr., until he died in a car accident in Mississippi. But when he was present, James was the personification of traditional masculinity. He loved and provided for his family. He showed no vulnerability, no tears. James's emotional expression lived in two spheres: sensual desire for his wife and anger at some disruption or injustice.

Lust and rage have always been hallmarks of American manhood. And they're supported by the assertion they are representative, too, of a certain kind of logic. They make sense. They're reasonable. They're certainly not womanish, which is limited to crying or hysteria. ("Hysteria" comes from the Greek, meaning "womb"—where life is formed.) We have decried and diminished women for how they express their feelings, how they expose their vulnerability. At the same time, we yell and scream and punch walls, all while complaining that women are "too emotional." We fail to see that our expressions of masculine rage are, in fact, emotions. And in our rage, we are never told that we are too sensitive or too emotional. As long as our only legible emotion is anger, we are never shamed.

These are the rules that I learned and spent most of my early life following. Religiously.

HERE'S WHAT I WAS *not* taught.

Black men model manhood after those who oppress us. We measure our humanity against the humanity of those who seek to kill us, our families, and maybe most of the planet. We imagine freedom to be the ability to accumulate the kind of unchecked power and privilege of cisgendered heterosexual White men. We eagerly embrace the toxicities of this conception of manhood: hypermasculinity, hypersexuality, homophobia, misogyny, and violence. Anytime we deviate from this script, we feel less masculine. And when we feel less masculine, we feel less human.

We swallow poison.

We embrace preachers whose theologies subordinate women and dehumanize Queer congregants. We venerate coaches who scream at us. We bond over fraternity rituals that require us to beat one another into brotherhood. We romanticize rage and the violence that accompanies it. Too often, our humanity is tied to our harm, our oppression.

Like the invented category of Whiteness, masculinity is an inherently corrupt idea. In the same way that I don't

want to recover or recuperate Whiteness, or reform or re-
build the police, I don't want to recuperate masculinity. Instead, it must be destroyed, along with all other frameworks
that prevent the full expression of joy, freedom, safety, self-
determination, and dignity. And for Black men, the stakes
couldn't be higher.

IT'S JUNE 2020 AND America is on its heels. Not just because of COVID-19, but because young people have taken to
the streets to resist state violence. I was asked to Zoom into
Drink Champs, a podcast hosted by rapper N.O.R.E., to dis-
cuss racism, policing, and other social issues. I was joining
N.O.R.E. along with rappers and activists Talib Kweli, Bun
B, and Mysonne. About two hours into the panel, an unexpected guest popped in.

Russell Simmons.

I was stunned.

Even before the accusations emerged about him, women
friends I knew and loved told me that he had sexually assaulted them. It had been a common story in the New York
media world that I'd come up in.

My blood boiled. Had I known that Russell was going to
be invited, I would have immediately turned down or can-
celed the appearance. I texted N.O.R.E. to express my frus-
tration and tell him that I needed to leave. He wasn't
checking his phone.

Nervous, I texted a friend for advice. What do I do? She
told me to stay but be careful not to affirm Russell in any
way. I did my best to avoid any contact with him or even

acknowledge his existence. Although it felt like an eternity, Russell left almost as quickly as he'd appeared. After the show, the host apologized for not telling me about the surprise appearance.

In the moment, I felt that I had done the best I could under unexpected circumstances. In reality, there were two options I did not exercise: speaking out right then or immediately leaving the show. Instead, I allowed my desire to be "professional" to stop me from going off script or leaving without notifying the host. And this is the ultimate embodiment of male privilege. As a man, I had the luxury of not having to make better, more responsible choices because I am considerably less likely to be harmed in the same ways as his alleged victims.

If a White supremacist had been on the show, I wouldn't have stayed. I would have voiced my opposition and swiftly removed myself.

Did I worry that speaking out against a man who had harmed Black women would make me professionally vulnerable? Would I have to relinquish some false sense of manhood? What is the cost of silence in the face of sexual violence against members of our community, against women, Queer folk?

At these moments, I realize that I have not come nearly as far as I would like to convince myself that I have.

AS AN UNDERGRADUATE AT Temple University, I was taking an unreasonable number of courses. I was committed to graduating that fall, but I needed to find one more class that fit my schedule. After checking the offerings from the African American studies department, I found the perfect option: a course called "The Black Woman." I didn't really have a sense of what it was about, but what did I have to lose? At the very least, I figured, there would be a lot of women in the class. And I was right. I walked into a room of brilliant and beautiful Black women and only one other brother.

The course was taught by Dr. Renoir McDonaugh, a Black feminist psychologist. We read scholarly texts like *Critical Race Feminism* and *Black Feminist Thought*, as well as novels like *Their Eyes Were Watching God*. The class radically shifted nearly everything that I thought I knew about myself, my sense of manhood. The work of bell hooks and Patricia Hill Collins helped me rethink my relationship to myself, my body, and the women in my life. For the first time, I learned to decenter myself and other male perspectives. I was unsettled in the best possible way.

I realized I was using my body in ways that weren't healthy for me. My choices weren't bringing me joy. In some ways, they were reinforcing my pain, the separation of mind and body. I was becoming emotionally void. I started reflecting on my relationships. I started to release the idea of healing through unhealthy means.

Sometimes men start punching things because we want to cry. We smoke, we drink, we have a lot of sex because we can't locate any functional alternatives. Growing up, I had to find "boy" things to do in order to feel like I was a whole person. It started as basketball, and then, as I got older, it was sex. I knew no other ways. What if there was something else?

Possibilities began to unfold about not only a different world, but a different me in that world. Exploring these possibilities made me feel both better and worse. Who had I been and who could I be? I started to feel vulnerable. Instead of running from that feeling, I doubled down and started going to therapy.

Today, therapy is a staple of my emotional diet, and I'm so much better for it. In the beginning, I saw it as a badge of shame, a sign of spiritual and psychological failure. Now it's a vital form of health maintenance. It's key to my survival.

IN ORDER TO UNLEARN unhealthy masculinity, we must run toward our fears. We must be willing to embrace the various forms of vulnerability that emerge when we disrupt the status quo. In my life, I've come face-to-face with the growing pains that accompany social, emotional, and professional vulnerability.

Professional vulnerability asks: *What jobs are you willing to lose?* Social vulnerability asks: *What networks and friendships are you willing to lose?* Emotional vulnerability asks: *Which layers of masculinity am I willing to shed in order to be a better—or really a whole—person?*

As a progressive man and someone who identifies as a feminist, I have done my absolute best to unlearn the unhealthiest parts of my identity. Through therapy, deep study, and engaged listening, I've unlearned the habit of restricting my emotions. At the same time, I have learned that I am allowed to be vulnerable, to be sad and in pain. I have come to think not individually but collectively, in community. This meant that I had to be accountable to people, as well as hold people accountable.

Accountability requires that I resist unhealthy masculinity in real time as it takes up space. For example, in academic meetings where everyone has a doctoral degree, my female colleagues are disproportionately asked to take notes. My job is to disrupt that practice by pointing it out, as well as making sure that I or another male colleague takes the notes. Romantically, it's making sure that my partner isn't doing all the traditional domestic work. Socially, it's speaking out against homophobia, hypermasculinity, and patriarchy in moments when it's so much easier to just be silent. It's creating space for my gay, lesbian, bisexual, transgender, and Queer sibs. I had to acknowledge that there are other ways to perform gender and masculinity. I had to unlearn traditional gender roles.

It's not enough for me to just not be homophobic. I cannot be friends with homophobes. I have to actually be willing to divest myself from relationships that are unhealthy. We all do.

When we're hanging in the locker room and somebody says something homophobic or when we are in the frat house and somebody says something misogynistic, we must be willing to speak up, even though there will be no social reward. And when the pushback comes, that's when we have to be willing to be strong. The people we're defending and the lives that we're affirming are more important than our social comfort. We have to be willing to detach ourselves from it.

It's easy for me to proclaim these values publicly, on a television broadcast or social media. I get all the benefits of being progressive when the world is watching. When no one is watching is when we are truly being tested.

Emotional vulnerability can cut deep. The world hasn't created space for us, particularly Black men, to say, "What you said hurt my feelings" or "What you said made me feel insecure or inadequate." "I miss you." "I love you."

These are things that we're not allowed to do. All of our emotionality has to come through the lens of those hyper-masculine traits like anger, violence, and sexuality. Sending a *wyd* text at 2:00 A.M. and saying "I miss you" are two totally different things.

Not believing that I had the space to be emotionally vulnerable is its own kind of pain. It kept me boxed in and prevented me from exercising the full range of who I am. It totally undermined my relationships.

In my twenties, dating was very difficult. I wasn't able to express what I was feeling. So I remained silent or distant. I dated a woman who often said, "You're not a connector." I didn't know what she meant at the time, but I've realized that because I wasn't able to connect, it made it much harder for her to feel safe, happy, and loved in the relationship. My emotional rigidity made it hard for me to love her well.

But when we're not emotionally vulnerable, we miss out on opportunities to have more authentic human relationships. It's harder to draw closer to our children. It's harder to draw closer to our parents. It's harder to draw closer to our romantic partners and friends. We never actually tap into the things that are bothering us or we're struggling with, because we can't acknowledge that we're hurt. We convince ourselves that we're feeling something different.

But it doesn't have to stay this way. We don't have to lose pieces of ourselves. We don't have to lose pieces of life.

I OFTEN REFLECT ON who I was as a little boy, before I internalized the belief that my sensitivity and vulnerability were legitimate sources of shame. Back then, I instinctively knew to follow my joy and be present in my feelings. I knew to honor what I felt, and I knew that I felt a lot. I knew that I was never too much. That what I felt wasn't too much. I'm trying to know that again.

I imagine a world where everyone has the kind of space they need to know their joy. A world where they can safely share their hearts. A world where their emotional needs can be met. And my freedom dreams are tied up with the project of dismantling any vision of manhood that limits or shames us. As long as we are not living in our full humanity, we cannot create a world for humanity.

The key to achieving this world is found in the practice. Having "good politics" matters, but so does our collective and daily labor. If we want more Black men to be vulnerable, we have to continue to show them how. We have to normalize telling people we love them and showing the men in our lives affection. If we want to produce newer and healthier forms of masculinity, those of us with platforms, power, and access have to continue to model it.

At forty-two, I'm watching a generation of people after me work to figure this all out. I want them to have corrected the mistakes my generation made and create new spaces for learning. It's happening. I'm beginning to see wider representations of masculinity, manhood, and emotionality.

As for me, I'm still, and forever, in process. I continue to see so many contradictions and places where I fall short. I don't see myself as an exemplar. I'm just somebody who's trying his best to figure this world out, failing every day but still committed to getting better.

A few weeks before writing this, I was doing a podcast talking about the tragic death of Kobe Bryant, whom I knew since childhood. In midsentence, as I reflected on the pain that came with the sudden loss, I started to cry. I couldn't have felt more vulnerable. But more important, I was completely okay sitting in that vulnerability.

Despite my considerable failures and contradictions, moments like this remind me that I'm growing and learning. Decades after being told I was too sensitive, I've never been more emotionally expressive or transparent. I've never felt more available to the people I love. I've never felt more healthy. I've never felt more free.

WE ARE HUMAN TOO: ON BLACKNESS, VULNERABILITY, DISABILITY, AND THE WORK AHEAD
—
KEAH BROWN

N THE SPIRIT OF HONESTY, I'M STILL FIGURING OUT what it means to be me. I know that I am a Black, disabled, Queer woman, and with that comes the kind of beauty, pain, joy, and exhaustion to which words can't really do justice. But I try anyway, because writing is one of the central ways I express myself. And self-expression is imperative to my survival. I am who I am—journalist, author, screenwriter; pop culture and fashion obsessive; cheesecake-loving, HomeGoods-swooning romantic-comedy aficionado—and I often find that writing about the things that make me me is how I make sense of the world and the people in it.

I also write to make sense of, reckon with, explore, and decide who I want to be in that world. I am a Black woman with cerebral palsy. It affects the right side of my body; I walk with a limp and have delayed motor skills as well as a limited range of motion. I've not always been proud of my disability. For the majority of my life, as I'd navigate public space, I'd curl in on myself with every passing stranger's stare at my hand or leg. I never wanted to be the center of their attention, and the gawking always felt like being told that I was what they considered "other." It also felt impossible for the gawkers to exist without making me feel bad as revenge for my disrupting their lives with my existence. I became ashamed of my appearance, of my limp, leg, and hand too.

But I have always loved being Black. In fact, the very first thing I ever learned to love about myself was my Black skin. As a kid, I'd watch Brandy as Cinderella—her beautiful blue gown the center of attention, the prince unable to help falling in love with her—and my mother as she would put on her makeup. I was in awe of the way we shared this beautiful skin, enamored with the idea that both a fictional woman and a real one could make me feel worthy, simply by having this one thing in common.

There was a time when loving and sharing my Black skin with these beautiful Black women was enough to keep me going, but at twelve, that stopped being so. As I turned my ear toward what my peers and society thought of disability, my own self-hatred began. A classmate made fun of me in the cafeteria, mocking the fact that I walked with a limp. For twelve-year-old me, the discovery of my disability as a bad thing was earth-shattering, fueling a self-hatred with the shame of being different, undesirable, and invisible. Long gone would be the days when my Blackness alone nurtured my worth.

The most interesting thing about shame is that it hangs around like all bad habits do, thriving on its familiarity, allowed to remain because we are either too tired or too jaded to think we can survive without it. I carried the shame that popped up in that cafeteria with me to high school, throughout college, and well into adulthood. Along the way I picked up the shame of being bad at numbers, of hating the way my voice sounded, of needing help, and of being what society told me was physically unattractive. I wished that God would spare me and I'd wake up the next day in a "better" body. From the ages of twelve to twenty-five, shame stole my ability to truly dream. I cared only about surviving and let shame convince me that no one genuinely cared about me.

What I did not know is that shame would still be there after I learned to love myself and my body. For shame switches tactics. After overcoming the initial shame of my existence, I didn't really want to talk about how I'd felt ashamed of my body and of being me. When I wrote my book in 2019, about my journey to self-love, I wanted to project that I'd always possessed this self-assurance and self-acceptance. But I had to tell the truth. And afterward, as you might guess, I felt more shame, for the person I'd once been. I'd gone from hating myself all those years to the embarrassment and regret of having ever felt that way in the first place, of having ever wanted a "better," more digestible body. Thankfully, though, God intervened. And as my profile began to rise—and I had to talk more about what it took to get to the side of self-love—I had to learn to forgive myself. I'd gotten pretty far in life with the girl I once was, so I couldn't begrudge and shame her now. I can only hope she sees the woman we are today and rejoices.

Now, at twenty-nine, I know shame will come and go, because the work we do on ourselves is a constant process.

"THE MOST DISRESPECTED PERSON in America is the Black woman. The most unprotected person in America is the Black woman. The most neglected person in America is the Black woman." Malcom X said it in 1962, and unfortunately, it still holds true today. We are often forced inside boxes and stereotypes—stoic and strong, never showing the toll that motherhood, sisterhood, spousal support, education takes on us. Change has to come, and not because we long for Black women to "save us" but because Black women deserve the chance to be who we are fully—magic, real, human— without apology or sacrifice.

THERE ARE THINGS THAT my body doesn't allow me to do, like walking long distances. This means I can't really attend physical protests, so I protest for change with the written word and across my platforms. I also fight by being all that I am without asking for permission. For instance, I like to say that there is a tear for every emotion and I can find them all: happiness, pain, anger. So I cry often. Not in front of others, aside from my therapist, but in the quiet of my room when night falls.

In February 2017, I cried tears of astonishment when the hashtag I created, #DisabledAndCute, went viral, global. I'd created it to help celebrate finally feeling good in my body, and to my delight, it is helping others do the same years later. Tears of relief, pride, fear, and anxiety came when my book was published. Leaving the set of the *Today* show after a promotional segment, I hugged my literary agent, carefully avoiding getting his shirt wet. Last year, when I modeled in a virtual fashion show aptly titled "Fashion Revolution" during New York Fashion Week, I cried when I saw myself on my computer screen strutting across my "runway" and giving the camera my best. When the show was over, I cried again, because no one can take that moment from me. I cried tears of joy once more after recording my TEDx talk, an event I thought would never actually happen.

Like most of the world in 2020, I cried tears of fear and worry, of loneliness from missing my friends and loved ones, wanting them to be as safe and healthy as possible. I have always operated under the idea that to cry and be emotional as a Black woman is an act of resistance. I don't subscribe to the idea that I can't be emotional simply because our society has no idea what to do with the genuine feelings and humanness of women. I will feel, be, and do as much as I want proudly for the rest of my life. To be vulnerable and emotional as a Black woman is to live in power, which I take back every day, not apologizing for who I am or the space I take up as I move throughout the world.

A reader once chastised me for using the phrase "what I know now" in my book. Their reasoning was that a twenty-seven-year-old (at the time) could not possibly know enough to "preach anything to her readers." As I write this, I think about that reader and how nice it is that they liked my book, but at the same time, I think it is ridiculous to think that talking about your lived experience is preaching. I don't have all of the answers, and I won't ever pretend to, but I believe that now more than ever, talking about our experiences is how we move forward. And honestly, I am tired of where we are. We deserve true, lasting change as a nation and the ability to exist in a world that sees people like me as full human beings.

I BELIEVE IN SPEAKING things into existence. I have spoken my literary agent and my first two books into existence. I spoke my film and TV manager into my life, as well as two cover stories, a *Today* show appearance, a first-class flight, meeting and becoming friends with my heroes, and modeling, among other things. I have never been shy about voicing my wants and dreams, of planning what the completion of them could bring about for my future. In those years when I stopped dreaming, I lost out on a lot, and so now, I work hard to make up for it. Dreams and wants are nothing without hard work, and when you have the added barriers that Black women often have, it is imperative to take the time to relish your dreams' completion before jumping on to the next. I know I struggle with sitting with my wins for a while, but I am working on that.

I am resilient because I am ambitious. I am resilient because every time someone has told me I could not, I did. Apart from rollerblading and riding a bike, I have taken "You can't" and laughed in its face. When my twin sister and

I were born five months premature, the doctors told my mother that we would never walk, talk, see, or go to a regular school, but we did. I want to be clear that none of those things is inherently bad but they show that I have been underestimated since birth. I am the daughter of Cheryl Brown and the granddaughter of Vera Mae Brown, two of the most resilient Black women I know. We lost my grandmother in 2009, and twelve years later, I can still feel her guiding hand when things get tough. My resilience is due to the care and love from these two women and from the Black women I am in community with and those who came before me. Growing up, I did not have the disabled representation I deserved, and so I try to be that for the disabled Black girls and women who are coming up so that they know anything is possible. Most of my resilience comes from my own determination to see a dream, a project, or a piece through.

My life has been a series of lows and highs, of rejections and acceptances, of grief and loss, of great music taste and hope. This sounds like such a cliché, but I am excited for the future. I spent so long thinking that things had to be perfect before I could make a lasting change, but 2020 shook that right out of me. I cried on my birthday out of gratitude for making it twenty-nine years on this earth. Through the wonder of technology, I survived and thrived, nurturing my relationships through and through during a pandemic. I raised my rates for writing and speaking, learning to value my time and expertise in a way that I was afraid to before. I said no to excessive free labor and yes to listening to my gut. I am still working on learning how to take breaks and days off, but we are all works in progress, right?

I am still figuring out all of what it means to be me fully. This will be a lifelong process, I am certain. But I am up for the task. With every vulnerability, every ounce of resistance and shame, with love of the Blackness, womanhood, Queerness, and disability in me, I am going to continue to show up for my people and, most important, myself. And I am going to look cute doing it. Because that is what I deserve.

WHAT'S IN A NAME?
—
LUVVIE AJAYI JONES

MY NAME IS LUVVIE. LAST NAME: AJAYI JONES. The Jones part is new.

I got married in September 2019. I had many important decisions to make, like how many people's feelings I was gonna hurt by not inviting them (weddings are expensive, and I love more people than I can afford to love). Another significant decision I made was to take on the last name of the man I married.

I took on the new but kept the old also, because whoever said you can't have your cake and eat it too never sat in front of good cake. To drop the Ajayi part of who I am felt like I'd be leaving behind who I've been. Which is strange, because this is officially the fourth name I've gone by. You'd think I'd be used to changing up my name by now.

I lowkey understand Sean John Puffy P Diddy Diddy Love Combs. Lowkey. Because sometimes, you are compelled to go by something new as your life journey moves forward. Lemme explain.

First, I was Ifeoluwa Ajayi. Then Lovette Ajayi. Then Luvvie Ajayi. Now Luvvie Ajayi Jones.

The immigrant. The scared new girl. The growing adult. The married woman.

I have made name switches in moments when I'm about to make leaps, often in fear and often quickly, as if my spirit knows it's time. And each instance has led to me meeting who I was meant to be.

My given first name is Ifeoluwa and it means "God's love" (*ife*–love, *oluwa*–God) in Yoruba. Shortened, it's Ife. For the first nine years of my life, that's what I went by. I am a child of Yorubaland, and in our culture, the names we are given lay the groundwork for a child who's entering the world. They are dreams for our future and are used to speak power into us and light our paths. My parents wanted my life to be anointed and led by love. So shall it be.

I was born and raised in Nigeria, and my family moved to the United States when I was nine years old. On my first day of school in Chicago, a city I had visited only once before, I felt strangeness for the first time. It was new for me to walk into a room where I was expected to belong, yet not everyone looked like me. It was my first time being "new." And it was the first time I felt like who I was just wouldn't do.

Coming from Nigeria, where everyone looked like me, spoke like me, and was Black like me, nine-year-old Ife was shook. Her usually solid feet wobbled a bit, and her self-assuredness hid behind her in fear. When I walked into the classroom, the teacher put me on the spot and asked me to stand in front of all these strange faces to introduce myself.

I immediately felt my tongue was too heavy and knew I was too different.

My name? I knew it wasn't welcome there. I just knew, because no one prepped me for this major change in my life and location. Ifeoluwa. *Ee-feh-oh-loo-wah*. Oh, it would be a tongue twister. The tone was also specific and it was too peculiar. It was too foreign, and it wouldn't do. So I introduced myself shakily as "Lovette" instead. It was a nickname that one of my aunts would call me from time to time. My given name felt like it was too much.

What I felt wasn't shame, because I was truly proud of my name. I loved it. I felt the need to protect a sacred part of me. So I decided in the three seconds after I was asked that I wouldn't let people in school have access to that version of me.

That is how Ifeoluwa Ajayi became Lovette Ajayi.

Having teachers look at my first name on their roll call list, then frown or say, "Whew, okay, this one is hard" affirmed my decision. And then having them butcher Ajayi (*Ah-jah-yee*) confirmed the message of "this thing about you makes us uncomfortable." I began to show up early on the first day of every year so I could go to each class and teacher and correct them before everyone else showed up. I told them to cross out Ifeoluwa on the list and replace it with Lovette. I didn't even want to deal with the public butchering and shame projection sent my way.

I settled into being Lovette quickly, as kids are adaptable. I chose her, and she was a necessary protector of my realm. At home, I was still Ife, eating her jollof rice and pounded yam with egusi stew. At school, sometimes I'd take sandwiches when I got tired of the kids asking, "What's that?" of my Nigerian food.

By high school, I had lost most of my Nigerian accent and didn't stand out much anymore because of how I spoke.

At graduation, we were required to be called by our legal names. Our school vice principal came to me a week before the ceremony and asked me to pronounce my name for him so he could get it right as I walked across the stage. He and I practiced my name for ten minutes. Whew, lawd, bless it. But it was worth it.

On graduation day, as I was next in line and handed over the card with *IFEOLUWA AJAYI* and its phonetic spelling written on it, my white vice principal saw my name, felt burdened by it, and said something that sounded like he was chewing gum. The only reason I knew he was referring to me was because there was no one in front of me. *Comme des fackons, dude. We practiced!*

Ugh. Just give me my diploma. This is why I'd revoked access to the use of that name.

Then I got to college, where the best learnings are outside the classroom. It was there that I met others with stories like mine, who also went by new names to keep theirs from being butchered. It was there where people heard my last name, and instead of tilting their heads in confusion, they beamed. "Oh, you're Nigerian! That's awesome!" College is where people can be different in a way high school doesn't welcome. And to find that community was an affirmation and an encouragement to use my difference as a superpower.

My first semester in undergrad, I took Chemistry 101, because, like the cliché immigrant kid I was, I thought I wanted to be a doctor. But, ummm, that dream came crashing down when I got a D. We thank God for some failures, because I don't even like hospitals, so I would have been, no doubt, the worst doctor ever.

Anywho, I started a weblog that semester. I think it was called Consider This the Letter I Never Sent and it was emo AF. And also terrible AF, because it was in Comic Sans. Bless my heart. Still, I fell in love with writing and maintained an online journal throughout my undergrad years. I was Lovette to my friends still, but some started calling me "Luvvie" for short.

When I graduated, I deleted that blog where I'd talked about the exams I was failing and roommate beefs, and I started a new one: Awesomely Luvvie. I decided to talk about the world as I saw it. I talked about race, feminism, shenanigans, and anything else I felt like. I wrote with a voice that was without pretense because I didn't think of it as anything but a hobby. I was working as a marketing coordinator for a nonprofit and liked it, but I would get home and write on my blog regularly. It was like a part-time job that didn't pay me.

Try as I might to insist that it was just a cute hobby that I had, my blog grew organically and started winning awards. More people started to know who Luvvie was than who Lovette was, and people started to call me a writer. Me. She of no couth who was only writing her opinions on a little website? *Me?* A writer? Isn't that what you call Toni Morrison and Terry McMillan? *Those* are writers. Yeah, so ain't no way I can be using the same title as them.

That was imposter syndrome speaking, of course. That hater-ass bitch. I had convinced myself that my version of writing, therefore my gift, was not extraordinary.

When I got laid off from my job in April 2010, I should have taken that as my cue to pay attention to this thing I was doing, but I still didn't give it credence. I looked for other jobs to no avail and would do freelance consulting to make money to buy shoes (cuz: priorities). There were times when I wanted to quit my blog, because I figured that I should probably put more energy into job hunting than this little website. But every time I'd want to quit, I'd get some press or an amazing note from someone who'd read my work saying what an impact it had on them.

In 2012, I got credentialed to do press coverage at the Academy Awards because of my blog. I got both red carpet and backstage access. I was in the room! I was eating all of Wolfgang Puck's catered shrimp back there instead of, you know, covering it, when it finally made sense to me. I'm a writer! My words got me here. I was standing next to journalists from CNN, the BBC, *The New York Times*. I was out of excuses not to declare it: I'm a writer.

Soon after, I was being interviewed by a journalist doing a feature on me and the (Not So) Little Blog That Could, and they asked, "How should we credit you for this? Lovette Ajayi, or Awesomely Luvvie?" I answered, "Luvvie Ajayi," before I could even think too hard about it. "Just Luvvie Ajayi is fine."

I had all of a sudden dropped Lovette. And it didn't jar me at all. Why? Because I knew Luvvie needed to move forward and Lovette had served me well. It was time. The woman who can say "I am a writer!" with an exclamation point, not a question mark. The woman who was scared of what it all meant but was excited to see about it anyway. The woman who knew her purpose was to move people with her words. She was here and ready to stand in it.

That is how Luvvie Ajayi came to be.

I decided to keep doing that thing that scared me, because on the other side of it would always be victory. I went all in on my purpose-driven life, to use my words to make people laugh, think critically, and leave this world better than they found it.

With that mission in mind, I wrote my first book, *I'm Judging You: The Do-Better Manual,* in 2015, and it was published in 2016. That book hit the *New York Times* bestseller list in the first week it came out. Changed my life. Because of it, I was able to fulfill my lifelong dream of retiring my mom. I called her a month after my book dropped and told her she never had to work again because I could officially handle her bills and mine.

My life has changed so much since, and as my career has grown, my personal life has also shifted. I met a dude, started dating him, got proposed to, said YES, and got married to him.

So on that day in September 2019, when I said, "Let's do

this life thing together" in my wedding vows, it signaled a shift in my priorities. I've seen myself go from the work, work, work woman to the woman who is now trying to find ways to focus more on herself. Family is now first, before anything.

I felt compelled to reflect that in my name. Which, for a recovering commitment-phobe and a fiercely independent goat, is a *big deal*. I even put it in my first book that my taking my future husband's name was not a given, because what if his last name was something like Focker?

Thankfully, I found me a Jones.

But was I going to take that name publicly and professionally? I wasn't sure. I was thirty-four when I got married, with a career that spanned sixteen years. I had a *brand,* y'all. A *brand*. Was I going to change that? Well, my brand is of someone who is authentic. And the real me knew I wanted to do it, but I was scared.

What was I scared of? Same thing I was afraid of when I didn't wanna call myself a writer. The title of "wife" felt so big, and although I was one, I wasn't sure I could live up to it. Hell yeah, I was scared.

So I did that thing I did with Lovette. I double-dutched between using Jones on professional things and leaving it off. For my speaking engagements or press mentions in the months following my wedding, there was no consistency. Sometimes I told people to use Luvvie Ajayi, other times I said Luvvie Ajayi Jones. It got confusing to me in a way that was familiar, and I knew I had to make a decision.

One day, my literary agent, Kristyn, called and asked, "What name should we put on your book cover?" regarding my second book, *Professional Troublemaker: The Fear-Fighter Manual.* I told her I'd call her back. Then I called two of my friends and asked them what they thought. They didn't give me the answer I wanted, which was firm direction. They simply said, "Well, what feels right for your book?" Me: "I don't know. That's why I'm calling you. Tell meeee." Nope. They did no such thing.

Wow. So I really have to figure this out on my own, huh? Adulting is a scam.

I called Kristyn, told her to show me two versions of the cover: one that said Luvvie Ajayi, one that said Luvvie Ajayi Jones.

So she did. And the only one that felt right was the one that said Luvvie Ajayi Jones. Why? Because the other one felt incomplete, as if it was missing something. It was missing the new version of me that I needed to own, fully, not halfway. I couldn't half-ass this, even though it was scary.

I called Kristyn and said, "Luvvie Ajayi Jones." I went on all my websites and changed my display name.

I didn't do it to prove anything to anyone, not even myself. I did it because everything in me said *DO IT.* It was scary, and daunting, and a *loud* proclamation of who I now was and one of the things I prioritized: the sacred space of my marital home.

It wasn't that I'd be *less* married if I'd decided to go by Luvvie Ajayi. The decision of what name we choose once married does not invalidate our commitment. But for me, like in the past, I knew that to be all in for this new season of my life, this was important for me to do.

I couldn't drop Ajayi, though. Across the years, as my

name has shifted, that has remained steady. That has an-chored me. I needed it to remain, to continue to tie me to my culture and lineage publicly, even as I created my own tradi-tions.

I also think about a little nine-year-old girl somewhere who is in a new land. Whose name is also heavy on people's tongues. I want her to have me to look to, as an example and an affirmation that her roots are worth keeping strong. I hope she hears my Ajayi spoken, and knows her diasporic epithet is worth celebrating, not hiding.

Besides, "Luvvie Jones" sounds very much like I'm try-ing to be nostalgic about a nineties romantic movie fave, *Love Jones*. Although it was the reason we made our wed-ding hashtag #LuvvJones (best wedding hashtag of all time, IMNHO).

I've settled into the woman I am, and into this marriage thing. My three-pronged name feels like a pair of shoes that are slightly too big because I still have much growing to do. And expansion can be daunting, but often, it is necessary.

I DON'T PLAN ON making another name change. Mr. Jones is stuck with me forever, and he is very welcome.

Ifeoluwa Ajayi made way for Lovette Ajayi to protect her-self in a new land. Lovette made way for Luvvie to claim her purpose. Luvvie Ajayi Jones has taken all the lessons she's learned from all of them and is the best version of herself she's ever been, wiser than ever and more grown than ever.

My names, all four of them, have been teachers for me, and I'm thankful for each of those people I was because they led to who I am today. And I'm thankful to my parents for naming me so well. The path of love they lit for me in my name has been a tool of resilience through any fear and an anchor through chaos.

The names we have tell stories, and mine speak of the journey of someone who has transformed so many times in her life, taking ownership of who she is in the world and creating sacred spaces for herself. My names have been my affirmation, and I'm grateful.

THE BLUES OF VULNERABILITY: LOVE AND HEALING BLACK YOUTH

—

SHAWN A. GINWRIGHT

UNCLE KENNY DIDN'T JUST LISTEN TO THE BLUES. He savored every delicious corn-battered, deep-fried lyrical nugget, the kind only Muddy Waters, Etta James, and B. B. King could serve. His cigarette would dangle from his lips as he flipped through his blues albums in the living room. I was only ten years old the first time I heard Bobby "Blue" Bland bellow out in his gritty golden voice, "They call it Stormy Monday but Tuesday's just as bad." Uncle Kenny was tall and dark, with beautiful bluish-black skin. "The blues is about life, the good and the bad," he'd say to me. I learned to listen, appreciating the deeply honest, soulful, vulnerable pulse of the blues.

The blues is about the soul opening up and pouring out whatever is inside—without shame, blame, or polish. Done well, it is raw, gutbucket truth-telling, but to get there requires a depth of emotional risk-taking and big doses of courage. The artist has to dive headfirst into some murky emotional waters with real honesty about the trouble that's been rattling around deep inside, and then put it on display for all to see. That's why we don't really listen to the blues, we feel them magically connecting to parts of ourselves we are afraid of, reminding us that we are human and struggling desperately, trying our best to be better. The truth is, there is power in our vulnerability; and our capacity to share parts of ourselves, even the parts we hide from, gives us enormous strength.

Black young people in America know the blues all too well. They feel the blues in schools that feel like prisons. They taste the blues each time a police officer stops them on the street. They can hear the blues every time they are turned away from a job. Black young people disproportionately experience higher rates of violence, poverty, and trauma than other racial groups. These traumatic experiences inflict a psychic wound that shows up as depression, despair, hopelessness, fear, anger, and pain.

Vulnerability can be one of the most important pathways to well-being among young people. When we lean into our own vulnerability with young people, it gives them permission to do the same. Just like the blues, vulnerability is emotional risk-taking, putting it all on the table and trusting that you won't be hurt when you do. Vulnerability is also the only way to form true transformative relationships because it raises the emotional stakes and creates a sacred agreement that what you just shared will be held and protected with tender care, without judgment.

I've worked with young people for nearly thirty years. My years of working with African American youth have taught me that we all have to play the blues every now and then. Emotional deception has no place in transformational work with young people of color. Those of us who work with youth know that the relationship is the most important intervention. That's why we have learned to "keep it real," and sometimes that means being vulnerable and letting our humanity spill out. When we do that, we make a sacred agreement weaving together trust and honesty, a brilliant fabric of authentic care, which is of course precisely what young people need in a world that shows them no love. How might we lean into vulnerability in ways that heal and restore young people's sense of belonging and well-being?

LIVING THE BLUES: TRAUMA AND VULNERABILITY

In 1989, I founded a summer camp for African American teens to restore their sense of well-being from living in highly stressful and violent neighborhoods and schools, a sanctuary for healing and soul restoration, and a refuge for the practice of vulnerability. Since that time, I've worked with more than ten thousand teens and I've learned a great deal about the power of vulnerability as an antidote to the trauma they've experienced. When a few college friends and I started the camp, we had no clue that so many young people were yearning for a space to laugh, play, cry, and heal. The depth and level of trauma young people were dealing with overwhelmed me, and I wasn't prepared to describe what was happening to our youth.

For example, I taught a session one summer about trauma and toxic stress and their impact on one's well-being to a small group of young people from Oakland. I explained to them, as I had been trained, the signs of post-traumatic stress disorder and what symptoms might look like. One young woman in the group calmly raised her hand and replied, "Ain't nothing 'post' about stress where I live. Something is always popping off." She was correct. The term PTSD was inadequate to capture the depth, scope, and frequency of trauma in her environment. For her, and many young people of color, stress is persistent, not post.

What she described was that trauma and crisis were commonplace in her neighborhood, and as a result, she and many of her peers had learned to work and live in persistent traumatic stress environments. Let me say that again. Persistent traumatic stress environments. There is an important distinction here. PTSE highlights the root causes of trauma, like food insecurity and lack of housing and access to medical care, while PTSD diagnoses only a "disorder" resulting from a past experience that is presumed to have concluded. African American youth often experience greater stress, anxiety, and depression because of the lack of safety, economic opportunities, and basic housing that are fundamental to well-being. Researchers, practitioners, and policy stakeholders all confirm that persistent stress has a negative impact on learning, healthy behavior, and mental health.

But young people don't describe what they see and experience every day like that. They just know that "something is always popping off." Yet the ongoing exposure to persistent trauma is devastating. I learned that firsthand working with Greg, a soft-spoken seventeen-year-old whose wide smile showed off his gold teeth. Greg's close friend was shot and killed not far from his home in East Oakland. Greg was there when it happened. When I asked him privately, "How are you feeling?" he responded precisely as almost every young man of color has when faced with a similar line of inquiry: "I'm cool, I'm good, I'm a'ight!"

The most egregious consequence of living in a persistent traumatic stress environment is the inability to feel. We know from research that emotional numbing is a coping mechanism to avoid processing the emotional turmoil. It's like hiding from your emotional self, stuffing all that emotion into a box, and tucking it neatly away down in the basement. When many African American youth experience trauma, they don't really have a way to get all the emotional stuff out of the basement. This is made even worse when young people lack the emotional vocabulary to name what's happening. I've never had a young person say to me, "I'm scared and frightened about what happened." Or, "I felt rejected and unloved when my father left me." So all that persistent traumatic stress stays inside, getting pushed further and further down.

The only real way to get all that emotional stuff out is to create an environment of safety and trust where young people can express what's on their minds and hearts. As Brené says, people have to earn the right to hear your story, and the only way to really connect with young people is through your own vulnerability, honesty, and rooted realness. It's sort of like playing the blues. You have to dig down deep, pull out things that you've been hiding, and put them on display.

PLAYING THE BLUES:
HEALING-CENTERED ENGAGEMENT

Healing-centered engagement is akin to the South African term "ubuntu," meaning that humanness is found through our interdependence, collective engagement, and service to others. The healing-centered approach comes from the idea that young people are not harmed in a vacuum, and therefore their healing cannot happen in one. Healing comes from sharing our stories and holding space to hear one another's pain, and joy, without judgment.

We know from research that healing is experienced collectively and shaped by shared identity such as race, gender identity, or sexual orientation. Healing-centered engagement is the result of building a healthy identity and a sense of belonging. For youth of color, these forms of healing can be rooted in culture and serve as an anchor to connect young people to a shared racial and ethnic identity that is both historically grounded and contemporarily relevant.

I've found that healing circles are an important feature in creating the space for communal healing. These circles create sacred bonds between people that are never broken, because when we are vulnerable in this way we can truly see one another. Similar to a disaster like a plane crash, or a natural tragedy like Hurricane Katrina, these events bring people together in profound ways, because our fragile exteriors are stripped away to reveal our raw humanity.

Healing-centered engagement embraces a holistic view of well-being that includes spiritual domains of health. This goes beyond viewing healing only from the lens of mental health and incorporates culturally grounded rituals and activities to restore well-being. When we sit together in a circle, we find commonality through our collective sharing. What makes this process so powerful is that we are tapping into collective pain and joy by sharing our experiences and providing the space to hold it.

FEELING THE BLUES: THE POLITICS OF VULNERABILITY

I'm guilty at times of running from vulnerability. Whoever is vulnerable, at risk, disposable, and dispensable is at the heart of the politics of vulnerability. Our identities matter, and safety about who we are vulnerable with is important. *Should I be vulnerable with white men who fear me? Should I be vulnerable with police who dehumanize me?* These questions are important for us to weave the connection to how vulnerability can cultivate healing-centered engagement with young people.

Studies of vulnerability, in general, have examined a range of disabling qualities and diminished capacities resulting from a place of helplessness or shortcoming. Brené Brown came along and completely changed the game, showing us the power that can come from discovering vulnerability in our personal and professional lives. But I'm also mindful that there is a politics of vulnerability when working with youth. Some of us can afford to be more vulnerable than others. Power, privilege, security are all conditions that can affect who is vulnerable, the consequences of being vulnerable, and what we gain from being vulnerable in our relationships with young people. So we also have to understand how issues of race, gender identity, social class, and power all determine the consequences of our vulnerability.

The blues taught me everything I needed to know about the politics of vulnerability, so let's return to the blues. The blues is an art form with roots in the Deep South. It is born from spirituals, chants, work songs, and field hollers created by enslaved Africans. The music evolved into revivalist hymns and folk music. At the heart of the blues are stories that convey suffering and joy, struggles and triumph, pain and pleasure. What makes the blues so powerful is that the artist can connect to the lyrics from some deep personal experience. So when B. B. King belts out, "The thrill is gone," he's singing from a lived experience, the pain of going through heartbreak and the joy of coming out on the other side. It's a type of emotional vulnerability. But the blues was also shaped by structural vulnerability, the laws, policies, and values that create oppression and suffering. The fact that the blues originated on Southern plantations in the nineteenth century is in itself an example of structural vulnerability. Structural vulnerability means that some groups in our society (racial, gendered, social class, religious) are likely to experience some form of social misery like poverty. Social misery is not just an individual experience, but a collective one. Yet these two forms of vulnerability (structural and emotional) work together. Structural vulnerability—poverty, gender marginalization, racial oppression—fuels and produces collective emotional harm and shared psychological injury, the ingredients for emotional vulnerability.

Now here is the point: In order to transform structural vulnerability, we need to tap into our emotional vulnerability. This is what I learned in my work with young people over the years. I have kept this in mind in all of my interactions with Black youth, personally and professionally. I always ask myself three questions.

BEING THE BLUES: CREATING HEALING-CENTERED ENGAGEMENT

1.   Am I practicing vulnerability in my relationships with people in communities I care about? Sometimes we engage in youth work from a distance, and are not close enough with people to practice vulnerability. Nearly every issue I care about—youth voice, racism, trauma, criminal justice—was born out of a deep relationship with someone who taught me more than I thought I knew about the topic. This meant sitting in a circle with young Black men on probation and listening to their stories, or spending time in a men's correctional facility and learning about compassion, or sitting at the kitchen table with mothers who are so stressed from daily doses of trauma. When we share our stories, we connect in ways that build bonds of understanding.

2. Have I created a safe container for vulnerability? Building the container for vulnerability is just as important as vulnerability itself. It's important to assess if it's relatively safe enough to practice vulnerability. This is tricky on the one hand because vulnerability, by its very nature, means social-emotional risk-taking. It means that there is something at stake when you share something that matters. On the other hand, if it is too safe, then there is no risk and therefore no growth in the relationship. The important thing to ask is, *Will I or could I be harmed by sharing this?* If the answer is yes, then you should rethink participating. But if the container is cultivated correctly, you'll feel safe enough to share because you've already considered if the person or group has earned the right to hear your story.

3. Can I make the adequate time commitment? Young people know when we aren't "keeping it real" and often feel disrespected when we fail to live up to our commitments. Your job is to first be honest with yourself about your capacity to go on the journey with young people. Once you make a commitment to create space to share their stories in an intentional way, this cultivates the healing we need in our work with youth.

We all have stories that can heal ourselves, young people, and our society. We just need the time and space to share them. So open up your favorite music app and listen to the blues for a while. You'll find that if you really feel, these stories of raw vulnerability can connect your own story of joy, pleasure, sadness with young people. These are the things that make us human, and if we make space enough in our lives to listen to young people, we can find the real secret to our own transformation, which is, of course, the only real way we change the world.

FILLING EVERY PAGE WITH JOY: REWRITING TRAUMA AND SHAME

KAIA NAADIRA

I CAN DO ALL THINGS THROUGH SPITE WHICH *strengthens me* was a motto I lived by for most of my life. I had pushed myself through high school and college and boys and girls and gender and Queerness by using my trauma as kindling for the massive inferno brewing in the pit of my stomach. I thought vengeance would save me. I was motivated by the constant thought of seeing my abusers, my harm-doers, watch me shine. And I wanted that shine to *burn* them. Resilience wasn't enough. Every time I got up, I was knocked down, or pushed down, or violated, or gaslit because I went into the world armed with only my strength. "Just be resilient," my mother always said. And I was. I held my chin up to the storm, but it still knocked me on my ass. I was living in a world that was constantly taking from me. My bodily autonomy, my agency, my joy—taken from me. So I clung to spite. I clung to my anger. And I gave it credit for every aspect of my success. I became obsessed with—and comfortable in—my bitterness because I somehow thought the reward would be joy. I ignored the rot and decay oozing from my spirit and learned to smile and speak and live as if I did not have this rage deep inside me. I felt myself turn to ash and float away in the wind. Deep down I knew the reward for my bitterness would only beget bitterness, because when you're living in rage, nothing is ever enough. Something is always *missing*. I wondered, If I did not have this anger living so deep in the pit of my belly and rooted in my soul, what did I have? What I should have been asking was, What did I *want*?

That was something I hadn't considered in years. I had no concept of what I wanted my survivorship to look like because the truth was, I didn't want to survive. I had always thought there was a cap on how long I could hold all this inside and still live. I knew I'd reach my breaking point one day, but until then I planned to patiently wait to die while engaging in as much recklessness as I could to speed up the process. My therapist called this mania. I called it life.

Not many people know about my diagnosis. I tend to place parts of myself, of my life, into vaults—locking them away to hide from the world. I always thought I had a certain air of general insanity about me. But being diagnosed with bipolar one disorder when I was just twenty-one was the nail in the coffin for me. I felt like God's favorite broken toy, because surely he must have been up there fucking with me. A life constantly *enduring* was not a life I ever wanted for myself. But what did I want? What did I need? The truth is, I had no clue. I certainly didn't expect the life I have. I didn't expect the trauma I would experience and eventually have to face. None of it. *Isn't it a drag that we have to pay the price for other people's hurt? That we have to bear the weight of the trauma they inflict on us?*

I suppose what I want is simple: I want a life and a body that feels like mine. I want to feel at home in myself. My goal for survivorship is to just feel whole. I don't feel like that's too much to ask.

WHEN I WAS ASSAULTED by one of my close friends, in an attempt to spare his feelings—and at my own expense—I downplayed the assault. "I'm fine," I told him. I assured *him* that *I* didn't feel assaulted. And at the end of our "conversation," I hugged *him* because it seemed right at the time. I should not have confronted him so soon, or on my own. I pretended I could be in his presence without feeling ill. That his physical touch didn't fill my whole being with disgust, with rage. The more I pushed these feelings down, the harder that fire in me burned, and somehow the person who deserved to see and feel that anger the most was never the target. Something about that filled me with more shame than my actual assault. Even if I could get over being violated, I could not get over the fact that I *let* him get away with it. I was disgusted by my own passive attitude. Why did I reach out to him? Why did I go to his room? Why didn't I speak up? Why did I continue to add to my burdens just to give him peace of mind?

I think I know the answer, but that's a hard truth to accept. The truth here in general was hard to accept. I had spent years dodging so many hurdles and carefully stepping around certain memories so that I never had to think about my first assault. I had carefully crafted myself into a person this could never happen to again. I was smart, charming, a perfectionist, wholesome, acceptably available but not so accessible that men could feel entitled, and yet here I was again. There is nothing you can do to take the target off your back when that is literally the way systems are designed. When you survive something once already, you'd think that would be the end of it, but somehow, despite all my work, I was here again. I'd rather pretend it doesn't exist than accept that. What I should have been blaming was a patriarchal society that does not focus on teaching people about consent from a young age. I should have been blaming a careless and thoughtless young man who actually harmed someone. But I was used to carrying way too much baggage and it was just easier to blame myself.

The shame over the price I was paying for the hurt other people inflicted on me, over the weight of the trauma they inflicted on me, led me to shut down. I was too angry to focus on school, so I dropped out. I was too angry to focus on living, so I stopped trying. I stopped trying to explore and find myself sexually because I had come to some deep understanding that I was never going to be a real person to anyone. I was a toy—a doll to be played with, undeserving of my own pleasure. I was simply to be used and discarded, and that made the rage inside of me swell even more. When I did speak of my assault—one of three times I allowed myself to name the harm inflicted on me—I spoke of it as if it happened to someone else, because I could not cope with the truth that I was now a two-time survivor of sexual assault. Imagine, you are a child with no understanding of the world, and the first thing you ever really believed about yourself was that you were complicit in your own abuse.

I was twenty-one the first time I saw someone face any consequences for causing me harm. During that time, a friend of mine got me a job at the club they were working at as a stripper. Before I went in for an official audition I decided to visit and see what a strip club was even like. I fell in love the moment I entered. In the center of the room was a stage with a scary-looking two-story-high pole flooded in red and blue lights. Not long after I took a seat at the edge of the stage, my friend went on. I was in awe of how confident and fluid they were. How they walked around the stage oozing sex appeal, commanding attention from every person in the club. I knew a few things to be true about my friend, the most important being that, like me, they were a dark-skinned nonbinary trans person. How could they, in this shrine to the cishet male ego, hold power? I had no idea how, but I was determined to find the answers, so I showed up the following Monday in my finest Victoria's Secret teddy and heeled boots, certainly not properly prepared but ready to learn the secret these women had.

Being a stripper was the best decision I ever made. And I'll say that with pride until the day I die. At a time when I was completely losing myself, stripping made me feel grounded. I learned to be bold and decisive. I became disciplined and I became so *fucking* confident. In stripping I saw myself as sexy for the first time. I felt powerful and capable. I learned to do exceptional things with my body. I could amaze a crowd with acrobatic stunts that seemed impossi-

ble to others but effortless for me. I could empty a grown
man's bank account in an hour and a half of pure fantasy
built just for him. I learned that the secret we as sex workers
have is that we are simply magicians. Despite what is weigh-
ing on our hearts and minds, we do our jobs and put on a
show. I was not the only one pushing through so much.
Through sex work I figured out that I am not flawed—I am
human. So I worked until the confidence and grace I conjured onstage could be conjured on demand, and from there
could just be a part of my daily life. If I could hold power in
there, I could have that power anywhere. That was the secret. Pole dancing was a huge part of the transformation I
went through that helped me discover myself as a person. I
came into this work with the same mindset with which I was
walking through life. I was just a toy, but at least I was being
paid for it. It was an unhelpful, and frankly toxic, mindset to
have when entering this field. *All the world's a stage, and all
the men and women merely tricks.* That's the motto. At
Fuego's I learned I was no doll. In a world ruled by cishet
norms, where cis male pleasure was centered, a Black, dark-
skinned, Queer nonbinary person managed to find and hold
power. Great power. I felt like I had turned the system
against itself.

Although I loved my job so much, I was still reminded
daily of the real world. During one of the slower days, I accepted a customer's request for a dance. He decided to pull
out his penis while I was dancing. I immediately dissoci-
ated. I could see myself falling through the sunken place
survivors know all too well—that place where we store our
deepest memories, that place where our triggers lie waiting

to absorb us into a state of paralysis. It happens so suddenly. Before I could pull myself out of it or curse him out, the club's security guards snatched him up and beat the shit out of him. At that moment I felt protected. It was the first time someone brought harm to me and someone else intervened. It was the first time someone else cared enough to act. This isn't to say that no one ever cared that I was abused, but it was the first time someone did anything about it. Watching that creep get grabbed in response to trespassing my boundaries was the most empowering moment of my young life.

Shame is a nasty feeling. It feels like being the spaghetti sauce–stained Tupperware in the set. Shame envelops your entire being and leaves you completely helpless. I never fully understood disgust until I understood shame. It's like this feeling of dread—like standing on a stage and watching the lights, every single one, turn off all around you until you are swallowed by darkness. Shame can feel like your greatest enemy and your only friend. Shame can feel like a burial for your sins—but you're the only one who cared enough to be in attendance. And shame can feel like a betrayal. A vicious and hateful betrayal that can't be forgiven or forgotten.

I was born Queer. I came out of the womb a brilliant and unforgiving burst of light with a rainbow beautiful enough to make God cry. While I never had the language to identify, I always knew who I was. I never knew it was something I had to announce until I was old enough to realize people talked and had opinions about business that was not theirs to mind. I was in eighth grade when I first felt the pull of what I believed to be love. She was a cute little church girl who gave me butterflies in the pit of my tummy. When her parents drove us to the church on Valentine's Day, we held pinkies in the back seat. It was our own little sign of rebellion, a silent revolution in the darkness. It was a harmless puppy love—two kids dreaming of freedom, life in the big city, new lives, adulthood, and a love we knew nothing of but were so incredibly curious about. I have never been the type to hide in the shadows about anything. I was raised not to. My feelings were my feelings and I felt them in their entirety. Then I shared those feelings at the kitchen table with my mother and my aunt. I didn't understand the fear—or the disgust—I saw until the weight of that shame hit me. I was not sure what, or how, but I had done something wrong. It was evidenced by the way my aunt leaned away from me immediately. It was clear in the way my mother spoke to me. In the silence that crept throughout the house in the days to follow. I had made a mistake, I had done something that made me wicked. I had committed an offense so heinous, my aunt never uttered a word to me again.

For a long time I was conflicted. I had been raised to be fearless and bold. I was taught to be unafraid of the truth and to embrace that actions have consequences. But when I spoke the truth, the consequences confused me. Was I wrong for being who I am and for sharing that with the people I love? I was told that I'd lose love, acceptance, religion, and family for choosing my Queerness. For choosing my happiness. At that moment I became afraid of the truth. I lived in a world where I was constantly ridiculed by the people around me. To be unaccepted by my peers, and then rejected by my family, was the worst heartbreak I'd ever known. I lived in fear of experiencing that feeling again. Shame turned my fear of rejection against me. I was afraid to share, afraid to open up, afraid to reach out—and especially afraid to trust. It wasn't that I lost the desire to, it was that when I tried my throat felt thick and the words felt impossible. I felt physically held back from speaking my truth. Even though I fought for my Queerness I still felt shame and fear.

When I came out as nonbinary at nineteen, I deeply expected the same reaction from my mother. But I was attempting to abandon my fear of the truth. I needed to be free. I was tired of living as myself *and* as the woman I used to be. That woman was gone by that point. But I knew that whatever dreams rooted in womanhood anyone had had for me were gone, and everyone else needed to know as well. Just like I fought for my Queerness, I would fight for my gender. Not many Black folks in my community know about being nonbinary. My mother had some understanding of it from (literal) arguments we had in the past about my then favorite rapper Angel Haze, an agender masterpiece. She also had a better understanding of it from her job at the time, dealing with Queer and genderqueer youth. Despite the progress I knew had been made, I was still terrified. What if I was pushing her too far? What if this was the thing that made her stop loving me? I pushed it aside, remembering that she'd always told me nothing I do could ever separate me from her love. And so I told her the truth. She stared dead at me and just said, "Okay, cool." That was it. The only follow-up question was, "So that's 'they/them,' right?" Somehow that scared me even more. I was already so defen-

sive. I could not understand why she was not. I had prepared myself for battle and she showed up unarmed, just
ready to love me like always.

There is no easy way to describe shame. In fact, most of
my troubles with this work came from trying to find some
easy but impactful way to describe this beast of an emotion.
Shame is sick and twisted, I know that. I know that shame
feels like an impossible labyrinth of misdeeds and bad
choices. But more than anything I know shame is a different
monster for us all. My shame is insidious. It stacks my mistakes one on top of another until I'm so overwhelmed I am
crushed by them, just suffocating under the weight. I think
worse than feeling the shame, though, is feeling the shame
alone. Just as much as shame is limiting, it's so incredibly
isolating. At least for me. And it's not just this feeling of no
one understanding what I'm going through. It's the idea that
no one will ever love me because of the mistakes I have
made. It is the lie I tell myself that because I have so many
skeletons in my closet, someone will find me disgusting or
unworthy. And I've stuck to this belief because it is the only
truth I've ever embraced. I am branded by my mistakes. I'm
certified damaged goods, and no one needs that.

I am still struggling now. Not in a grand or intense way,
but a silent tug-of-war in my subconscious. I was recently in
a toxic, abusive relationship. In this relationship I was with
someone who lied to me and emotionally manipulated and
gaslit me. They eventually put their hands on me. It isn't
something I'm proud of. When the abuse began, I kept that
side of them from my friends. I was never a dull person and
deep down I was aware I was being manipulated. But when

you've spent most of your life embracing the idea that every-one is always going to hate you, and any suffering you en-dure is punishment for one of the countless wrongs you've committed in the past, it's hard to believe it can get much better. I was twenty-one and in love. In love with an idea despite their many empty promises, despite what they showed me to be true of them. And when you are in love, you stick it out, you fix the problem, and you fix them. And I was going to fix them because *I* was beyond saving. For nearly eight months I ignored friends who saw the red flags and begged me to realize I deserved more. I dealt with em-barrassing outbursts in front of friends and told them the same excuses I told myself. "They're just like that some-times. We're working on it." "They've got a lot goin' on. I'm sorry, y'all."

This may be my biggest skeleton. How do I explain to people whom I want to date moving forward that you can-not touch me suddenly because I will panic? How do I ex-plain that I am absolutely terrified when someone yells because I'm unsure of what will happen next? How do I ex-plain when the next person I date claims they'll never hurt me that I don't believe them because memories of the past constantly repeat in my head like a broken record? Because the last person who claimed they would never hurt me pushed my body to the ground and kept me there until I agreed to stay with them. These are not things you over-come easily, and so I keep that close to my chest. Because when I try to share them, that choking feeling comes. My throat feels impossibly small, and I close back up. My body won't allow me to let it out or let it go.

The truth is, I will always be a survivor. I will always wonder who I could have been if I had not been so traumatized so early. There will always be something that I will have to overcome, and truthfully I think that's okay. Being a survivor is now a badge of honor for me. I can say with pride that I did more than power through and I'm doing more than surviving: I am living. At least I'm living life to the fullest I can. Vengeance is not my savior, because I saved myself. Dancing saved me, my community saved me, love saved me. When I shifted my thinking a little bit more from a victim mindset to embracing survivorship, I had so much more respect for the strength I had shown, but I also realized that it was time to stop carrying everything alone. My Queer/ trans family saved me more than anything. I am eternally grateful for the chosen family that saw me at my lowest and still loved me. For people who showed up whenever and wherever without complaint. Without them I never would have realized that I wasn't alone. Without them I would have never released the death grip I had on my anger and started really thinking about what was next for me. Thanks to them I have an entirely new blank chapter to write, and I plan on filling every page with joy.

HONORING OUR STORIES, TRANSFORMING OUR PAIN

—

DERAN YOUNG

WE DON'T TALK ENOUGH ABOUT RACIAL TRAUMA in this country. In fact, even as a therapist and facilitator, I found myself stunned one fateful day when my son came home from kindergarten crying. When I asked what happened, he replied, "I wish I was white like everybody else." I froze. I didn't know what to say or do. I thought to myself, *When did this happen? How did this happen? What did I miss?* I spun into a shame-guilt spiral: *I'm the founder of Black Therapists Rock, for goodness' sake! I've really messed up somewhere along the way if my own kid wants to be white.* My son further explained that during recess, one of his white friends didn't want to play with him and said, "Brown kids aren't as fun as playing with other kids."

A few hours later, after recovering from the shock of this statement, I hid in a corner to wipe my own tears, and slowly regained my parental bearings. I realized that what mattered most was that he was able to give words to his sadness. Even at his young age, he was able to do something that I struggle to do as an adult—he spoke truth to power. The last thing he needed was for me to be overwhelmed with shame or guilt. What he did need was for me to be with him in this familiar yet overwhelming pain so that he didn't have to carry it alone. I needed to not only reaffirm his inherent worth and value but also validate that what he had experienced was racism and that it was not "just in his head"—it was real and so was the emotional impact. I'm glad that my son trusted me with his pain and felt connected enough to share his experience. The very definition of trauma is that we are in it alone, with little or no emotional support to make meaning of critical, life-altering experiences.

Together we did some deep breathing and grounding, and I realized that he had activated the little girl in me who probably experienced a similar feeling but had to hide it. Growing up in Wichita Falls, Texas, where the KKK had held quarterly rallies and publicly burned crosses as a form of visual intimidation, I had learned to cope through silence. My mother was extremely pro-Black (but definitely not anti-white; she was more pro-people). She talked about historic Black leaders constantly. I believe this may have been the saving grace of my race socialization. However, because we were surrounded by violence and chaos in the projects, on top of her personal struggles with drug addiction and untreated mental illness, I felt she didn't have time to be bothered with my "little feelings" and questions about my environment. So I did what most of us do. I learned to numb my feelings so that I could work "twice as hard" to make "something of myself."

Working twice as hard leaves us chronically exhausted, and emotionally unavailable to ourselves or anyone else. We then raise children who feel emotionally neglected. As a mother, I acknowledge the emotional weight of parenting Black children. I imagine it's the same psychological burden our enslaved ancestors carried.

Racial trauma is the psychological result of having to navigate white supremacy culture in a body that is made to feel inferior. It makes us feel trapped in our own skin. It makes us feel as though we are suffocating and choking on hundreds of daily messages filled with shame. This includes humiliating events at work, having to have "the talk" with our teenagers about driving while Black, and the vicarious trauma of witnessing public murders of Black and Brown bodies. Collectively, we armor up to function in this environment, leaving the trauma misunderstood and misdiagnosed. This protective armor creates steel cages around our hearts and significantly reduces our capacity for healthy connections, both inside and out.

We can't live a wholehearted life without connection. Experiencing love, joy, belonging, requires us to be *with* our feelings. We can't heal if we continue to pretend we aren't hurting. Hurt people hurt people. In America, because of our history, we are all hurting. As a country, the story we collectively make up is that feelings and people don't matter. We turn to this story because believing it is easier than the risk of feeling and connecting.

When we don't have healthy connections, we learn how to navigate the world in isolation, which isn't really living—

just merely functioning. Sometimes I talk about vulnerable things but don't allow myself to feel vulnerable.

If it's not connecting me to more of who I am, if it's not coming from this deep, vulnerable place in my heart, is it really connection?

If it's coming from my head or if I have an agenda behind it, is it really connecting?

Certified Daring Way Facilitator Dr. LaDonna Butler states, "Vulnerability, the state of showing up, unarmored, shaking, yet willing to embrace the benefit and consequence of human relationship, sometimes feels counterintuitive as a Black person. Our collective internal protection mechanisms are transmitted strategies of survival that we inherited from our ancestors. However, vulnerability in the face of racial trauma challenges the operating systems of oppression. It illuminates the sheer Power of our presence. The Truth of our existence as equitable partners in humanity."

When I'm being vulnerable with myself about all of my life experiences, I remember why I had to armor up in the first place. By honoring my pain, I can take inventory and decide which of these methods of protection I need in this moment and which I can leave behind. I have more choices and more liberation around how I show up with other people.

Racism threatens our ability to set healthy boundaries by silencing us and calling our experiences and realities into question. This is especially true when you grow up in poverty or when there are multiple layers of oppression like homophobia, transphobia, fatphobia, ableism, sexism, classism, Islamophobia, or xenophobia. The layers of "otherness" smother and silence our voices. Through this silence other forms of trauma go unchecked and unspoken, including multiple forms of abuse.

In recent years, I have learned what it means to "go inside," and I realized why a part of me felt that it was dangerous, overwhelming, and inconceivable because of my childhood sexual abuse. Sexual abuse robs us from connection to ourselves, especially to our bodies. When we become disconnected from our bodies, it impacts us throughout life. When we live in households filled with shame, there are secrets we hold, and we are taught to ignore whatever it is we think we need, especially when we need help. Living in a Black body, asking for help is one of the most vulnerable things we can do.

Code-switching, which I learned to do very early in my life, is a survival strategy that requires you to push away parts of who you are and over-function in other parts. We create all these roles to try to control the impact of racism, to tame it and change ourselves. Trying to get on the "good side" of racism by being the "model Black person." There are so many things that we do to shape our whole lives around these internal messages of "you're not good enough" and "you are unworthy." Carrying the burden of silence, racial trauma, and shame is exhausting and soul-crushing.

Shame resilience, according to Brené Brown, "is the ability to practice authenticity when we experience shame, to move through the experience without sacrificing our values, to come out on the other side of the shame experience with more courage, compassion, and connection than we had going into it." We can affirm ourselves once we realize that we are inherently worthy of basic human rights, and we begin to understand that the system is sick, not us. Critical awareness and the intentional refusal to internalize oppressive messages are necessary to develop shame resilience.

In my work, I have found that it is very common for Black people to think that discussing emotion is selfish and a waste of time. Why? Because it is not going to change my reality. It is not going to put food on the table. It is not going to help me survive. A lot of times we think, *I'm feeling sorry for myself and where's that going to get me? I am just going to feel more victimized if I actually allow myself to feel these things.*

That is the fear—that the emotion will take over or overwhelm us. That we will lose emotional control. That's a very real fear when you still have to wake up in the morning and pretend you're not depressed, worried, or outraged. We think we're going to get stuck and drown in it and we're going to be overwhelmed by it. Who has time for that? Ain't nobody got time for that.

When I advise someone to go to therapy, or talk about feelings, or even just journal, my recommendations are often disregarded, because I am retired military and have all the privilege and economic access that comes with being middle class. I understand that many people feel they are too busy working to keep food on the table and a roof over their heads and trying not to get shot by the cops. They often feel most of their time is focused on just trying to survive and there will never be any time available for them to be vulnerable.

However, scarcity is a mindset that there will *never* be enough. It goes beyond our present experience and projects forward to wreak havoc on our future long before it arrives. Anytime you hear the words "should," "never," "can't," or "always," look for raw materials of scarcity: shame, comparison, and disengagement.

External constraints are very real for the 8.1 million Black Americans living in poverty. Even among the middle class, some are just a few paychecks away from being homeless. Because of the very real poverty brought on by generations of systemic racism, many of us are brought up to believe that vulnerability is a costly privilege that we simply can't afford to give to ourselves or our loved ones. So we hide behind our shame shields, attempting to protect ourselves and one another. A life filled with fear and hypervigilance makes it difficult to trust anyone, including ourselves. A lot of us don't trust our family, our parents, or other Black people. We have been taught that Black is bad or wrong, and we often carry this self-limiting unconscious belief about ourselves and one another.

Shadawn McCants, another certified facilitator in The Daring Way, explains it as "a legacy burden that makes it hard to 'kumbaya' in a world that hates me for the color of my skin, the texture of my hair, the bass in my voice, and the will to want to live the American dream." In white supremacy culture, it's a dog-eat-dog world, and everybody is fighting for as much privilege as they can possibly get. Vulnerability is seen as weak and for suckers.

Acknowledging the impact of racism on your life is like

walking into a big dark murky cave. You know that once you go in there, you're not going to be able to see, you're not going to know where you're going or what you'll find. But you walk in anyway because you know there are things in that cave that you need to reclaim, things that have been taken from you. You walk in, despite the fear, to reclaim your ability to speak up and say what you need—to be seen and heard, and to take up space.

As a Black woman, it feels like an act of resistance to have an intentional life—to say that my life is going to be meaningful, to live out the mantra of Black Lives Matter. Living in constant fear that your life could end at any moment, your future orientation is cut short and the capacity for hope is often reduced. I have great compassion for the parts of me that didn't want to hope or dream because they carried a deep fear of disappointment. I had to admit that deep down inside, I had been carrying years of anger and despair.

Patriarchy has created a culture in which men aren't allowed to feel and women are often punished for doing so publicly. Avoiding emotions has resulted in abuse of power in many forms and at many levels. In our facilitation training we talk about how it's very difficult to ask people to set down their armor and be vulnerable when racism and white supremacy demands armor. We talk about how this is especially true for Black men. I've been pondering this statement and I've actually been asking Black men what they need for their healing.

Here is what Ty Cutner, a men's personal development

coach, shared. "I can't name a lonelier, less cared for, more feared group in America than the Black man. The stereotype promoted in the media for hundreds of years has been that the Black man is dangerous. Is it possible to build a relationship with someone you consciously or unconsciously fear? Black men even fear each other, reducing the chances of emotional connection, trust, social support, or community. We live in a country that's hostile toward us, increasing our loneliness. We don't feel valued when we can't provide for our families, and since our ability to provide is limited, we often carry a sense of low self-worth. Most of us are extremely lonely. Who can Black men truly be vulnerable with?"

I think the answer for all of us is that we have to start by owning our pain and being deeply vulnerable with ourselves first. We must each uncover our own inner wisdom. This is what the Sankofa means to me. *Sankofa* is a word from the Twi language of Ghana that translates as "Go back and get it." The Sankofa is a metaphorical symbol used by the Akan people of Ghana, generally pictured as a bird, with its head turned backward taking an egg from its back. It expresses the importance of reaching back to knowledge learned in the past and bringing it into the present to make positive progress.

I believe we should all honor and be amazed by our own stories and the connected heritage of those who came before us. I'm amazed that *all* of my ancestors survived long enough for me to simply exist in the world! The struggle and hope that allowed me to be here means that my life has meaning and it matters. Maya Angelou said it best: "I believe we feel safest when we go inside ourselves and find home, a place where we belong and maybe the only place we really do." This is where our vulnerability starts—in the home inside of us.

During my childhood I experienced frequent relocations and long periods of homelessness. I didn't have the sense of home that I'm having to create as an adult. As descendants of people who were stolen from their homeland, we often have difficulty finding our way back home. In 2009, I made my first of many trips to Ghana, West Africa. Something inside me healed when I walked through the Door of Return, a monument that acknowledges the destruction of the transatlantic slave trade. Living in Ghana for six months the following year was the first time in my life that I experienced a deep feeling of community support and consistent joy. I was home. Physically and emotionally.

I believe that corrective experiences and relational connections outline the path of healing. When I went into the slave dungeons in Ghana, I remember putting my hand on the walls and purposely and intentionally wanting to bear witness to the suffering of our ancestors. This deep-seated pain that we collectively *still* carry in our DNA is rarely acknowledged and has yet to be accounted for and repaired. For me, reparations would be fully funding our healing.

When I came back to the United States, I knew that I wanted to help more Black people experience joy and pride around Blackness in the midst of white supremacy culture. I created the nonprofit Black Therapists Rock six years later to start to create community and connection among Black healers, who often are dealing with their own racial trauma as well as professional isolation. One of my favorite quotes is an African proverb: *If you want to go fast, go alone. If you want to go far, go together.* We must come together to heal. Our village is counting on it.

RUNNING OUT OF GAS
—
SONYA RENEE TAYLOR

I N EARLY DECEMBER 2012, A MONTH AFTER MY MOTH-
er's death, I sat in Sean's tight kitchen, my wide hips spilling
over the sides of his sleek chrome stools. Before me, swirling in the belly of a spotless wineglass, was a Cabernet-
Merlot blend he had poured generously from an elegant
carafe. Sean always poured his bottles of red wine into ca-
rafes first, so they might "open properly," as he put it. The
walls of the kitchen were a bright sunflower yellow whose
contrast against the carafe intensified the blood plum color
of the wine. I lifted the glass from the table, stared into its
deep garnet well, and thought of my own hauled blood flow
each month. I thought of my mother's blood that once emp-
tied out with the new moon just as my own was soon to do,
as her mother's had done and her mother before her and so
on—a legacy of emptying. I thought about how I had rested
in Terry's womb as she rested in her mother's womb. How I
had always been with my mommy before she was even fully
with herself. Then I thought of the mortician draining the

rich red wine from my mommy's body before filling her with a foreign mephitic liquid. Something that likely tasted of toxins and tannins.

My mother died on a Thursday in late October but began dying long before that. We hadn't spoken regularly in months. Not since she started drinking in the mornings, making my "Is she sober?" calculations unreliable. We were the same woman, Terry and I, always looking for a way out of ourselves inside something else, whether it be brown liquor or brown bodies. Too often, this is what the world gives Black women: escape hatches to nowhere. Tunnels that empty into our same fractured lives. Rarely any routes to care or a soft someplace, just the thud of falling back into the same shit we've been trying to get out of. My mother and I were a mirror loop of shame, circling our own addictions only to end up staring at the other, which was to be staring at ourselves. I'd spent every year after my tenth birthday patchworking an identity that might one day make my crack-addicted mother stay and care for me. And Terry spent every year after my tenth birthday running from the demons that made it impossible for her to care for her children. In our loops, we just kept running into our fears and away from the one thing that might have saved us both: love.

Sean stood in front of the stove stirring the onions and potatoes he was preparing along with the prime cuts of steak on broil in the oven. He was not a man fluent in the verbal exchanges of intimacy, but for nearly twenty years Sean had cared for me like this, with wine and dinners. Short, dark-skinned, impeccably groomed, well dressed, good smelling, he fancied himself worldly, a Renaissance man. I would not begrudge him the title. My first dining experience at a restaurant with white linen tablecloths and coiffed male servers who pulled out my chair and rid the table of breadcrumbs using little plastic shovels happened on a date with Sean. He was a Black man who introduced me to discriminating wines, authentic reggae, and morbid videos like *Faces of Death*. In the early years of our friendship we would lounge on the couch of his college apartment and watch these twisted videos—a cocky skydiver descending over a river of alligators, only to short his landing by a few feet and wind up chum in their snapping jaws. Two bottles of wine and six "captured on film" deaths later we relocated to his bedroom and unceremoniously had sex. The sex occurred as an act of happenstance in our friendship—like a side effect of our genitals being in a shared vicinity. Getting naked was never presented as the intention of our time together—to consciously pair sex with our friendship would be to admit we were more than friends, admit we owed each other some truth. Neither Sean nor I was in the truth-telling business.

I suppose it was ironic that we met as coworkers for a teen pregnancy prevention and education peer program. We were nineteen and twenty, both hired to teach safer sex, communication, and decision-making skills for middle- and high-school kids. A staple of the curriculum was role plays designed to help students differentiate between passive, aggressive, and assertive communication styles. Sean was often cast as the aggressive boyfriend attempting to pressure me, his pretend girlfriend, into being sexual with him. My task was to use my assertive communication techniques to defuse the peer pressure. Sean reveled in his villainy, committed to fraying my assertive reserve. He played dirty—stuffing grapes from the day's lunch platter in my mouth midsentence while moving his body so close to my own that the electric field of our attraction would short-circuit my access to language. He was a farceur—a master persuader who made me feel luscious and wanted. In the blurred margins between role play and reality, in front of a classroom full of eighth graders, I decided I would start fucking Sean.

Sixteen years later, Sean and I still resided in the same nebulous expanse between friend and fuck. We never discussed the sex we had, neither before nor after. This day would be no different. The end of 2012 was a dying clock, each second seemingly slower than the preceding one. I had five weeks before I was scheduled to move to California. By the time Terry died it was agonizingly clear that nothing would keep me from throwing my body on top of and beneath anyone who might press out the grief. I was stringing together multiple states and placing them between me and every reckless decision I had made since the day the mortician handed me a pile of gray-white gravel and ash in a plastic bag, inside a square black container, placed in a white cardboard box heavy as a small toolkit, a box filled with a woman named Terry Hines. A woman I used to call Mommy.

Driving to Sean's house in Philadelphia was an act of harm reduction, a last-ditch effort to kick the jones for the person I most desperately desired to let destroy me, Kwasi.

For three years I screwed Kwasi to abandon myself, like my mother had abandoned me. I was at Sean's house for the same reason I would have gone to Kwasi's, but Sean was a lesser drug, methadone instead of heroin. Regardless, every person I'd ever slept with was supposed to replace my mother. They did not. And tonight I was going to let Sean inside me because my mommy was dead in every city of every nation on the planet and that truth bulldozed me. Because she left me at center stage in all my shit and nothing to hold on to but her ashes. I slept with people, all sorts of people, because it was what I'd learned to do with a sorrow in the marrow of my bones . . . try to disappear it.

I was starving. Sean would feed me, not this meal he was preparing, though it was a kind gesture. Food in the past eight weeks had been reduced to a gauze-flavored substance people foisted on me then watched me eat. Eating was the evidence I provided to concerned friends that I wasn't passively trying to follow Terry to wherever she had gone. No one seemed to realize I had been secretly following my mother's dead-end directions long before her earthly departure.

The tined blade of each day without her peeled me. Raw and ravenous for any sensation to eclipse grief for even an hour, I shuffled the meal around on my plate and waited in agitation for the formality of dinner with Sean to end. He watched me in confusion. "Why aren't you eating? Damn, Sonie. I have never seen you like this."

"Sean, my mother is dead. How else would you expect me to be?"

"Yeah, that's true."

His considered tone intimated that perhaps he had forgotten that small detail. For all his debonair stylizing and feigned arrogance, it was obvious Sean felt minified and impotent beside the monument of sadness I had become. Grief had carved me into a new edifice and grief had hollowed me out. We finished the meal in relative quiet, crawled into bed, and hit the light switch. Sean moved his hand toward me, disrupting the dark pocket of silence between us—a movement as predictable as death or love. He slid his cool palm inside the T-shirt he had given me to wear to bed—another formality—then grazed the tip of his index finger against my nipple. Here was the invitation I had come all this way for—a meal he'd offered me many times before. And without a word, I ate.

The next morning, Sean made me coffee, poured it in a metal travel mug, and walked me downstairs to my car. His stiff hug was just as awkward as it had been for sixteen years. "I hope you feel better." He held open the car door as I climbed inside. He turned toward his house and disappeared behind the paint-chipped white plywood door. I pulled out of the driveway and down his narrow street. By the time I got to the first stoplight, I was hungry again.

Leaving a D.C. work meeting a few days after my visit with Sean and a week past Thanksgiving, I headed down New York Avenue toward Route 50 and the Baltimore-Washington Parkway—toward what should have been a straight shot home. Instead, I made a left-hand turn on Minnesota Avenue. This rerouting was as outside of any conscious machinations as blinking or swallowing. It was automatic. Going to Sean, feeding the hunger, had turned

over an ignition inside me—one I had no key for. I was a rev-
ving engine, a car stuck in drive. I would not stop until I ran
out of gas. Here I was, not wanting to, but nevertheless driving north toward the D.C. neighborhood of Columbia
Heights—toward Kwasi. I looped 16th Street through Harvard Street with its shoddy and souped-up brick homes set
back far enough for the inhabitants to have fenced front
yards, then drove back up 14th Street past 7-Eleven and
Target, then across Park Road and over to 16th Street again.
I studied the profiles of Black men's faces in the dark along
the way. *Is that a goatee? No, his beard is too thin.* I examined their frames, quickly excluding those whose bodies
rose above six feet. *His pants are too tight. He is walking
too fast.* I performed this ritual of circle and investigation,
identification and elimination no fewer than ten times for
the next hour looking for Kwasi. I finally pulled my car in
front of Marx Cafe off 16th Street, parked in the No Parking zone, and screamed in outrage, "FUUUUCKKKKKK
YOUUUUUUUUUUU!!!!!!!!" to an entity that was both
me and Kwasi and God and no one. And the engine in me
and me inside my car both sputtered and stalled—my tank
finally empty.

To the left of my car the restaurant bar pulsed with
strange bodies I could see through the glass front door—
D.C. newcomers sipping Cuba libres and taking swigs of
craft beer under the titian lights. Marx's served as evidence
of the ever-lightening complexion of Chocolate City. A
white-owned Communist-themed bar in a Brown neighborhood, indifferently belched up from the gut of gentrification

without so much as an "excuse me" to anyone. My self-righteous judgment did not stop me from routinely sitting at that bar opposite Kwasi, watching the contours of his hands and mouth as he courted then swallowed his glass of Maker's on the rocks—as I took deliberate sips of vodka tonic with a squeeze of lime just before we ambled our way back to his attic or basement only a few blocks down the street.

As was our cycle, Kwasi had stopped answering my calls shortly after I visited him with my mother's cremains in tow. He did as he said he would that day—fucked me like my husband—but he had no intentions of treating me as such. Initially, I feigned gratitude. His rejection was helping me prepare for my move. He was doing me a favor by extracting himself from my life. For the first few weeks after that, I made myself busy with online Bay Area house hunting, re-searching moving companies, and being ambushed by sor-row nightly. When the hook of sadness hitched itself to my chest and towed me through the day, I would masturbate before bed to augment the pain with some facsimile too flat and gray to call pleasure—but better than the hook. Soon the facsimile rendered itself useless—the week it stopped working, I drove to Sean's house. I fed the beast, and now, outside the Marx Cafe, it would not stop growling at me from inside my own belly.

I sat in the car seething and buckled under my own lack of self-control. Even still, on a muted internal channel I con-tinued willing Kwasi to actualize off of 16th Street in my blurred field of vision. My phone rang abruptly. The sound of the ring tone physically hurt—an unwelcome auditory pinch that shoved me back into my body. I fumbled through my purse and answered.

My therapist, Dr. Byron, was calling, as she did several times a week since my mother died—an extension of care far beyond her therapeutic duties. There had been a rotating cast of therapists over the years. A series of fits and starts that were as much a function of my unreadiness to face the emotional closet collapsing in real time under the weight of my self-delusion as they were a result of a host of professional ineptitudes and mismatches. Neither my inability to cease sexual relations with Kwasi, nor my mother's unwinding thread of sanity chased by Seagram's gin, led me to the couch of the middle-aged ginger-haired woman with long limbs and gracious eyes. Flight anxiety was what finally forced me into therapy in 2011. I began having full-on panic attacks prior to boarding planes. I took two flights a month on average and much of my income depended on air travel. Not until my trauma began to edge itself into the territory of my fledgling economic security was I even remotely willing to peek at it.

For the first year, I saw Dr. Byron weekly, mostly over video sessions, but she called daily the first two weeks after Terry died, when I was in Virginia. She talked to me for an hour as I stood in a public laundromat, washing and folding the thirteen loads of flea-infested, mildewed shirts, sheets, and socks left abandoned in my mother's laundry room, some sopping and soured in her broken washing machine. The fleas were the remaining evidence of the lonely desperation that compelled her to take in a stray dog a month before she died, a litany of beginnings and tragic endings. Dr. Byron accompanied me as I navigated the mundanities of death and the bureaucracy of dead-people business. Later I would share with her how death dragged madness out of me—how I sat on my bedroom floor for two hours, my hands plunged wrist-deep into the container of ashes in my lap. How I felt possessed by a compulsion to scoop up two palms' worth of my mommy's gravelly bone fragments and eat them—to be full with Terry. Dr. Byron was the only one who knew in graphic detail how I wanted to—was willing to—put anything in my mouth, anything in my body to fill up the nothing. Dr. Byron knew a part of me had died with my mother. She knew, when I did not, that a part of me needed to.

"Hi, Sonya. How are you?" she said. "I don't know, Dr. Byron," I replied, jaw still tight with anger that my diablerie had not conjured up Kwasi. I lied to everyone but her. Each week she presented me with a bowl empty of reproof and teeming with grace. Despite my best efforts, I could not help but pour honesty into such a sacred container.

It took me a year into our sessions before I could look her directly in the eyes. She would say, "You are lovable, Sonya."

And I would bow my head like a serf at such an implausible idea. During an appointment, I told her I felt indomitably unlovable—that even she loved me only because I paid her.

"No, Sonya," she said. "You pay me for my time. You do not pay me to love you. I choose to love you."

Dr. Byron is where I tried on intimacy like I tried on my

mother's heels as a child—the shoes flopping about on my tiny feet, so much space to grow into. "Dr. Byron, I have been driving around in circles for an hour trying to run into Kwasi," I said. A flush of shame followed the words.

"What is it that you want from Kwasi, Sonya?" she asked.

I started to say, "To screw, duh!" when I caught my own lie and swallowed it midsentence. I wanted Kwasi to do the impossible. I wanted him to fill the hole. The empty in me was an entire planet, a solid celestial body insistent on being acknowledged. My sortilege did not summon Kwasi. It summoned only my acute awareness of the complete globe of nothingness, an impermeable mass that had taken up residence in the negative space where my mother used to live. Nothing could be done with the whole/hole, but I drove in circles for an hour praying someone—not someone, Kwasi—would split the grieving world of me into manageable pieces. "I want him to . . ." The rest of the sentence was atomized in a planetary collision of mourning. My chest heaved as I bayed into the phone.

"I know, dear. I know. You miss your mommy." For fifteen minutes my therapist rocked me feather-soft on the other end of a phone while I howled and cursed a world devoid of Terry. And as quickly as a blackjack dealer might flip the final card in a hand, laughter turned me over. How absurd I must have looked, menacing D.C. in the dark stalking short Black men.

"I must sound full-blown crazy. I have really been lurking around D.C. like a stalker tonight. And two seconds ago, I was in hysterics. Dr. Byron, I am losing it."

"No, you are not, Sonya. You are simply in this new moment. Grief was here. Now, in this moment, there is laughter. You can welcome both."

In the first months without my mom, I was learning how to be with both. How to be with all of me—the whole. I ended my call with Dr. Byron and started up my car. I drove toward Baltimore. It was 9:45 P.M., time to go to bed. I looked down at the fuel gauge, slightly concerned. No worries. I would make it home—my gas tank was full.

MY JOURNEY: VULNERABILITY, RAGE, AND BEING BLACK IN THE ART WORLD

—
IRENE ANTONIA DIANE REECE

AM A CONTEMPORARY ARTIST AND VISUAL ACTIVIST, born and raised in Houston, Texas. My work is cathartic. Each series I create is a call and response for the memories I have experienced in my life. The journey of my work thematically brings my Black identity to the center stage. My Blackness is not linear, it is fluid. Being Black is multifaceted and I want to show all of it. I want to continue to eliminate the normality of the one type of Black person that is showcased in white-centric art institutions. Interacting with my family archives became my sanctuary as a child. Reliving and rememory of the images allowed me to heal. Later in my career I was drawn back to my family archives, this time using them as a form of activism and celebration. Throughout this passage I am giving you permission to see my emotions and experience what I experience. What I experience in these photographs is love, grief, rage, and joy. The art that has been created and showcased in this book is unending, it is forever growing with me—spiritually and physically. I imagine years from now, whenever I am physically unable to hold a camera or make art with my hands, I will go back to these bodies of work, much like my family albums, to find resolutions for my everyday life and continue to heal.

Billie-James series, KIN, 2019, inkjet print with dried flowers

I was abroad in grad school when my father called to tell me his sister Yogie, my auntie, had died. Being alone, hearing my father's voice, and trying to be strong brought back old wounds of my granddaddy's (my father's father) passing when I was nine and pulled me to my family archives repeatedly. I held on to this portrait that had my deceased loved ones in it—its warmth and vibrance offering me endless waves of comfort. Feelings of grief, memory, and love came falling in when I started to work with the materials. I covered my loved ones' faces with flowers at that moment, born of the pain of missing them and the tenderness of remembering them. I wanted to be able to express myself, this time as an adult versus when I was nine and unable to. We weren't ever taught to grieve, only to be sad and then never talk of the pain again. Whenever I have these moments to myself to listen and take in the photographs, I feel myself letting go of the pain of missing them and wishing they were here.

Looking through archives has power. I believe it can be used as a form of activism and healing. Particularly the picture in the center, of my father's childhood birthday party. Throughout grad school, I found myself dealing with instructors, guest curators, and peers displaying pure ignorance toward that image. A lot of people thought I staged that photograph. I then was confronted with the reality that they had never seen a Black family portrayed with full-on Black joy. I remembered saying to them, "My goal is to break down the canon, the white gaze. I want to continue to make work for my communities only, so this is my way of doing so. People need to be exposed to these circulations of fluidity

My family archives, photographic archives
courtesy of Dorothy and Garry Reece

that Blackness holds. It should never be viewed as something linear." That obviously struck a nerve with them. I
came off combative, but I was—I was fighting to protect my
family archives, to protect my Black identity. It's hard to un-

learn whiteness when it's being pushed on you your whole life as a "good thing," especially in art institutions and universities. For mainstream media, the imagery of Blackness has been controlled and contrived into how white folx view our community. I'm in control of my narrative, and I'm going to tell my story.

My childhood consisted of dancing Ballet Folklorico and reciting poems of Langston Hughes to my father and mother while screaming, "I'm Black and I'm Proud! I'm Mexican and I'm Proud!" My childhood was peculiar growing up in a biracial household. My mother is Mexican American, my father is Black, and both grew up in small rural towns in Texas before they met in the middle of Houston. My father was very vocal about embracing Black identity. I saw myself being around groups and people that embraced my mother's features and culture instead of my father's, and this impacted my childhood. Due to my father uplifting my Afrocentric features and ideology, I found myself mirroring him when creating art with a heavy sprinkle of Black intersectional feminism. I often get asked why I haven't made art surrounding my Mexican culture or heritage. It's not that simple for me. The same way I was asked to choose between my identities growing up, I get berated in my adult life as an artist for not doing enough work about my Mexican side. What is it they want me to create? Latinidad doesn't celebrate or acknowledge Black or Indigenous Latinx folx and, based on my experience, I have to first make work about how Latinidad has impacted me. I have tried to separate the two identities but it causes more harm than good, in my opinion. I refuse to make art under the false romanticiza-

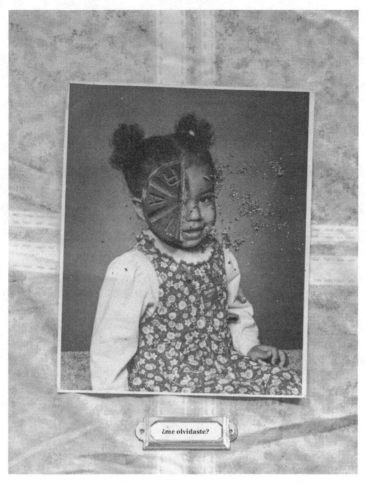

¿me olvidaste?

"I know we don't talk about it but, we should" series,
You Know We Are Related, 2020, inkjet print with a
label and Mexican hot chocolate piece

tion of Latinx culture. In talking about my experience of my
Mexican side, my Black identity will always be part of that,
and that's the part they don't want. I continue to give them
what they don't want, by speaking from my Black experi-

ence growing up around my Mexican family and friends from the Latinx community. We really don't talk about white supremacy and colonialism much with our family, especially on my mother's side.

I was accustomed to masking my pain through my work. As a twenty-seven-year-old, I have recently made some reflections on the trauma that appears throughout the body of work *oc·u·lus* /'äkyələs/: the recurring violence in the United States' medical system toward Black lives—especially Black women and Black children being misdiagnosed. The photographs on the next page represent a moment in time of me being vulnerable. I was diagnosed with a prolactinoma pituitary tumor at the age of twenty, during my freshman year of college. I was told that I was born with this particular tumor. It first appeared with five-hour nosebleeds, with me stopping up my nose with cardboard from the toilet rolls, and then hours of joint pain. My vision shifted. I needed glasses but no one believed me. I was told time and time again I was seeking attention. By the time high school came around, I was defeated. I developed major symptoms: unbearable pain and lactation. I kept those a secret for four years because I didn't have the strength to defend myself, to be shot down for attention-seeking behavior once again. I found myself creating an art piece to make my voice heard: "I experience pain. My pain is real—I am human—I matter—I matter!"

I started using the mixture of archives and the creation of my own photographs initially to find answers about myself—partially to heal. Digging in boxes, finding albums tucked away in closets, some that were tossed aside in the

nevertheless you tried your best
to stay a kid. the growing pains
grew more painful. and the crying
for help stopped because no one
believed you anyway. you were
just a kid that everyone thought
you were seeking attention. and
when you became a teen everyone
thought you were just acting out,
or having sex, or doing drugs.
and so when you became a woman
you just stopped asking for help.

oc·u·lus / ˈäkyələs/ series, You were a kid (top)
and Time to take your medicine Bean (bottom), 2020,
inkjet prints with cabergoline medicine

trash because they were building up mildew, as if they were
meaningless. Remembering memories, remembering our
histories, holds joy and deep heaviness for my community. I
look at this picture of my ninety-one-year-old granny and

I Look Out For Mine series, Granny & Bean, 2019,
silver gelatin (digitally modified)

me. She has done everything to shape me to be the beautiful Black woman that I am. I think of the generational love and resilience each picture holds in my family albums. As I continue this journey of working with my family archives to create acts of healing and to end generational trauma, I think about our past, the African diaspora—the erasure of us. The gestures I made restoring, circulating, and archiving them felt metaphorical, like bringing their souls back. I did it to protect not only the physicality but the spirituality. I want my kin to know: I know you exist. I promise I will never forget you. I will always love you even after you are gone, and I will continue your legacy of protecting our community through resilience, love, and rage.

UNLEARNING SHAME AND REMEMBERING LOVE
—
YOLO AKILI ROBINSON

> Sometimes I wake up and have to remind myself:
> There is nothing wrong with me. I have patterns to
> unlearn, new behaviors to embody, and wounds to heal.
> But there is nothing wrong with me and the core of who
> I am. I am unlearning generations of harm and
> remembering love. It takes time.
>
> —YOLO AKILI ROBINSON

WAS SO EXCITED WHEN TARANA APPROACHED ME TO write an essay. Not only was I honored, but as a wellness practitioner who has worked in Black communities for the past fifteen years, I felt like I had so much insight to share.

The night I started writing this essay, I just knew the words would fly through my fingers. I was ready to tell it all: how I saw forced gender socialization as a tool that creates shame, how I saw homophobia as the heart of male violence against women, how ableism and assumptions of normal keep us struggling with our differences. **I was ready.** But the moment I opened up my computer to start typing, I felt this sharp sensation pinch me in my gut: **Something was not right.**

My first reaction was to try to push past the feeling. So I started to come up with a few academic terms, even wrote a few paragraphs that would make a sociology professor proud; but nothing landed. What I was offering was not embodied and I felt the emptiness echo from the page. I kept asking myself: *Why? Why am I having so much difficulty with this? Why is writing about this so hard?*

Finally, after two nights of not arriving at a discernible draft, I gave in and decided to take a break. Almost immediately after I stopped, my internal shame narratives started rattling off in my head: *Maybe I can't write because I need rest. Maybe it's COVID brain. Maybe I am not the person to write this and I have gotten in over my head.*

I decided to close my laptop. "I will revisit this in the morning," I told myself.

But before the light from my MacBook could fade, the tears started streaming from my eyes. I started sobbing. Snotty, mouth-wide-open sobs that prompted me, even alone in my apartment, to instinctively look around to ensure no one was seeing me ugly cry.

I cried because I knew I was not ready to write about shame.

And that I couldn't write about shame without writing about me.

Shame is defined by Brené Brown as "the intensely painful feeling or experience of believing that we are flawed and therefore unworthy of love, belonging, and connection."

Using this definition, I realize that I have never known who I am without shame. As a Black nonbinary Queer person born in America, I have never had the privilege of experiencing shame as just a feeling. I, like so many of us, was introduced to shame from birth as an intrapsychic and systemic reality. I was branded with shame by virtue of my Black skin, wide nose, and limp wrist. I was indoctrinated with shame from the history books to the media to my communities' unanswered demands for justice.

So in order to speak of my own shame, and of shame and Blackness, I need you to first understand that through the lens of white supremacy, being Black is shame. And how we struggle to love ourselves and move through that shame is synonymous with how we battle white supremacy.

II

One of my earliest memories of shame is from when I was six. My father, who then served in the military and lived in Germany, had come to Fort Lauderdale to visit me, my sister, and my mother. We lived with my maternal grandmother, Lottie May Cuyler. My father was tough and taut then (he is a Taurus), muscles and shiny boots wrapped in the green and black camouflage of his military uniform. He came to Florida to find me, limp-wristed and light-footed (a Libra), hanging on the hem of my grandmother's dresses, enamored by her and the women who ran my life and what I saw as their everyday magic. He was not pleased. I believe he was worried for me. Worried for my survival in the rough world we lived in as poor Black folks. Worried that I would be destroyed, killed, ridiculed for my fairylike nature. He was likely right. But whatever he felt at that time, what I felt from him toward me was disgust. I remember him looking down on me, his face scrunched up, the sun shining high behind him in the sky. He was clearly perturbed with my mannerisms and affect. I can hear him loud as day yelling at my mother: **"He needs to get from 'round all these got-damn women!"**

What my father could not know was that those women— his wife, my aunts and grandmother—were my everything. And when I heard him say these things it made me feel ashamed for loving them. For desiring their wisdom and presence. For wanting to be like them because they were the only stable thing in my world. Too many of the men I knew were like him: in rage, disconnected, swirling tornadoes of unpredictable chaos. I understand his rage now as pain, his attempts to stifle my expression as caution. However, my little mind could not make those distinctions then.

In the way many of our caregivers' voices do, some of his shame became my own internal voice. The voice that would never allow me to receive compliments, because I didn't work hard enough. The voice that would not allow me to receive love, because I was not good enough. Too soft, too wrong, *too always around all those got-damn women.* I hear the same thing from men, gay and straight, to this day. It is this shame voice that materializes through men in my life and has all too often made more sense than love and affection—because it is more familiar.

Shame untreated stifles love.

Shame through the years has led me to excuse abuse and patterns of harm, because I didn't believe I deserved much more. My interpretation of my father's actions, and the shame I experienced with them, pulled me continuously into reenacting that narrative.

Shame unhealed is an intergenerational curse.

III

"How dare you not be strong? How dare you not be together? You should be ashamed. You have slept in bed for days. Black people are not this way. *You* don't get to be this way. How dare you be crazy, unkempt, reckless? How dare you not know all things? *How dare you not be an unfeeling animal, unfazed by the woes of the world? Who told you that you had the right to be white?*"

White supremacy shames us out of our humanity and programs us to shame one another at its service. The cotton-field culture of slavery meant we were forced to push through rain or shine, sickness or health, because failing to do so could mean the death of those we held dear. Like so many patterns from slavery, that pattern persists in Black mental health today. Researchers have called it John Henryism. The concept that we can, and must, push through to reach our objective, and that no pain matters in the process as long as we reach our goal. This attitude has real-life consequences: It impacts our ability to own our depression. It stigmatizes folks' experiences with psychosis and mania, linking with other legitimate fears of psychiatric care that

Black folks have, creating a pungent mixture that prevents us from engaging interventions that can save our lives.

IN OUR COMMUNITIES, the historical shame about not "keeping it together" for white perception also manifests in the way we are trained to "be respectable or die." Some part of the cultural Black psyche still remembers the core roots of this respectability:

"Put that face up and smile when that white man spits in your face. It is not safe to scream or attack him in anger."

"Hide your sister away when she screams out in the night, running from visions and monsters only her mind's eye can see. Don't you speak of mental illness. Don't you let them know she's touched. What they will do to her will be far worse than any danger the cotton fields can ever measure out. I don't wanna hear no talk about mental conditions. Mental conditions are for humans. And since when have the white folks let us be that?"

IV

To be Queer, trans, and Black is to know that when you are walking in Harlem, men will turn to look away from you, 'cause to look at you is to see their shame. Their whole lives it has been beaten into them that anything is better than being like **you.** Don't worry, you will get accustomed to the hurried rushes when you approach. You will learn to pretend you don't hear your cousins' side conversations about your sins. The words of Black women, bustling by whispering your existence is a "waste," will wash past you on the streets and become as mundane as the smell of flour at the fish fry, as normal as the bodega cat climbing the shelves. It will pool together and prevent your wrist from relaxing, curb the twitch in your walk, or lead you to raise your jaw up so high to hold back the tears.

Shame sits in the body and restricts the flow of love.

V

For Black Queer men and nonbinary folks projected as men, gay culture is an ongoing competition to see who can shame whom first and with the most power. We are trained to seek out emotional intel on others to exploit vulnerable and private moments. We are trained to dig into information about sexual prowess, dick size, ability to take dick, or if one has a dick. We are trained to scour the details to find a flaw, femininity, any opportunity to lift ourselves above one another and build a poisonous patriarchal sense of self-esteem.

Shame has also trained us to secrecy, because to thrive we learn to lie at such an early age.

"You got sugar in your tank, boy?"

No ma'am.

"You ain't gay or nuthin', are you?!"

Hell naw!

When you are raised to lie and hide to survive, if you are not careful you will learn to lie and hide to live. In Queer culture these patterns of lying are so persistent that when you challenge them people think you are being homophobic.

We lie and hide to survive because we know that all too often when we are seen, we are thrown away. We learn early on from our communities that our sexual expressions are not desired, our bodies are not desired, our patterns of loving are not what our loved ones want. This leads to both shame and an obsession with being wanted that contorts our ability to cultivate intimacy. So we try to gym the shame away. Orgasm and ejaculate the shame away. Church it away, smoke it away, meth it away, anything other than look at it directly and face its enormous power. Heterosexism, transphobia, and homophobia hold us hostage in a structural web of hate we conflate with community.

Shame restricts the imagination and creates the illusion that it is culture.

VI

Surprise!

White supremacy is not responsible.

You are not poor because of systems. You are poor because you did not pick enough cotton.

Shame.

Surprise!

White supremacy is not responsible.

Your friend is not dead because the system teaches men that trans lives are comical and disgusting. They are dead because you didn't do enough to protect them.

Shame.

Surprise!

White supremacy is not responsible.

Black folks are not distrustful of mental health because of the trauma they face within the system. They are distrusting because they don't respect that they are white folks' test subjects.

Shame.

Surprise!

Black gay men don't have higher rates of HIV because the system never fully funded Black gay HIV/AIDS institutions. It's because Black gay men were confused to think their lives matter as much as white gay men's.

Surprise!

Surprise!

Surprise!

But is it *surprising*?

Systems of white supremacy teach us shame because they have no guilt.

Rejecting shame for Black lives means rejecting individual responsibility for structural failures.

VII

For too long shame has been a central organizing force in Black communities. We have used shame to motivate people to go to church. To vote. To control women's bodies and sexual desires. To toss away our trans and gay children and take roles in institutions that tear our communities apart. To transform shame in our communities, we are going to have to weed it out. We are going to have to find a way to express our concern that doesn't equate to our noses in the air or our backs turned on our ugly. We are going to have to chant from the street corners to the halfway homes, from the ERs and the encampments to the church pews and the house and ball competitions, to every Black life we come across: *Shame is not your name. Shame is not my name. There is nothing wrong with you. There is nothing wrong with me. We have patterns to unlearn, new behaviors to embody, and wounds to heal. But there is nothing wrong with us and the core of who we are. We are unlearning generations of shame and remembering love. It takes time. And the time is now.*

HURT PEOPLE HURT PEOPLE
—
LAVERNE COX

I DON'T KNOW HOW TO LEAVE MY FRONT DOOR AND not armor up. I'm becoming aware of just how automatic it is for me. And it makes me really sad, because I would love to let it go.

I had surgery earlier this year, and about two weeks afterward, I had to go to the pharmacy and pick up a prescription. This is in Hollywood. It was my first time leaving the house after surgery and I couldn't walk fast. I felt vulnerable. It was scary because my way is to walk fast and to always look around me, hyperaware of my environment. Because I've been kicked on the street. I've been harassed. All kinds of shit has gone down.

And that day I was coming back from the pharmacy, wearing my mask and a visor, and this woman says, "Hey, sister. How you doing? Oh, excuse me. I mean, brother," and totally misgenders me. Still today. This happened this year. I often associate the misgendering with danger, because I don't know what's about to happen. And I was thinking, *I can't run, I can't run now, I can't* . . . I was so terribly scared. I'm forty-eight, I'm famous Laverne Cox. And I'm still scared to leave the house. I'm scared of walking down the street, because it's still not safe to be a Black trans woman just walking down the street.

So the armor. The armor is real.

My great-grandfather was a freedman in Alabama. One day, he was walking around Selma and saw this dead cow on the road. This would have been the early 1900s, I think. He took the dead cow home, cooked it to feed his family, and everybody got sick. But apparently that dead cow belonged to some white people. The white people tracked down my great-grandfather and put him in jail for taking a dead cow off the road. And then once he was put in jail, that was a way to sell Black people back into slavery. They called it share-cropping but it was forced labor. And so then he was sold out of jail into indentured servitude. My grandfather—J. P. Cox—was born on the plantation, where he was essentially kept a slave years after emancipation. He and my great-uncle Reuben didn't like to talk about it, but they were beaten to make them work. It was deeply traumatizing stuff.

My grandfather was a son of a bitch. He beat my grand-mother. He cheated on her. He was abusive to the kids. Some of my mother's brothers and sisters have a different memory of that, but my mother tells harrowing stories of domestic violence that my grandfather perpetrated. He had his affairs and never brought money home. The lights would be turned off. All kinds of really fucked up, traumatic shit that my grandmother endured, that my mother endured.

The compassionate part of me thinks, *Where were the tools for my grandfather to process having been beaten on a plantation?* He passed his trauma along to his kids, and they were traumatized. And my mother, bless her heart— we've worked through a lot of this. She's seventy years old now, but my mother was emotionally abusive. She just was. What else did she know? How do we reckon with the story, as Brené says, not just of collective trauma but of historic trauma? How it's not just passed down in our practice but passed down in our genes.

Violence is violence. Most of the people killing Black trans women are Black men. And I am not saying this to demonize Black men. I don't want to participate in that. But it's the reality. Let's just talk about what's actually happening. The venom that I've experienced from some other Black folks has often felt like, *Oh, this is a disgrace to the race.* That my transness as a Black person is a disgrace to the race. And that's some white people shit. That is the historic trauma of not the figurative but the literal emasculation of Black men in America, something that we still need to unpack and heal from.

When Black men were lynched, their genitals were often cut off, pickled, and sold—a literal emasculation of Black men. It happened. And then there's me, a Black trans woman, a person who's assigned male at birth. I've often felt the historic trauma of the emasculation of Black men that some Black folks have projected onto my identity as a trans woman. But my transness is not a result of white supremacist oppression. Trans people have always existed.

There's just so much trauma so many of us don't know how to acknowledge, let alone cultivate resilience around. But if we don't talk about trauma, if we don't talk about shame and do the work to begin to heal, to develop shame and trauma resilience, we can't fully come together.

I think many of us are in so much pain, so much hurt. What I've been trying to show is that that pain, that hurt, is intergenerational, it's historical, and it's collective. And hurt people hurt people.

There is a lot of shame. Shaming people for their skin color, for their size, for the way they talk. Classism, colorism, misogyny. It's all intersecting. And so it piles up. The work must be to understand that these things are structural and then we must begin to do the work to stop internalizing all of it.

I didn't just solve my internalized transphobia five years ago and now I'm good. It's something I still have to work through. It's something I work on every single day. My internalized racism and classism are issues I have to confront in various ways at various times. It's never comfortable. These things are so linked to trauma pathways and neural pathways in my body; these things are so deeply ingrained. Creating new, more resilient pathways, new ways of thinking and acting, takes consistent practice.

I don't believe we can have conversations about racial justice or gender justice or class justice if we don't talk about shame and trauma. I don't think it's possible.

It's actually necessary.

BLACK SURRENDER WITHIN THE IVORY TOWER

—

JESSICA J. WILLIAMS

WRITING IS THE PLACE WHERE I HAVE ALLOWED myself to become most vulnerable. From a computer, I type with my eyes closed and almost in a trance. I allow my words to come, sometimes despite my outlines, planning, and internal editing. I don't know what I feel until I read what I have written. The words that arrive are the ones that simply have to be heard. I surrender to them.

Surrendering has become one of my favorite practices. In considering how to begin to tell a bit of my story, I had to return to the familiarity of my ritual to remember to trust my own process. Several now-deleted drafts prior, I was too distracted by performing—allowing my mask to speak for me instead of trusting my own voice to narrate. After each draft, I convinced myself that the editors would read it and determine it was a mistake to have invited me to contribute. I feared not being good enough, or being "found out" somehow, as if I had not earned the right to speak or, if I am being truly honest, had not earned the right to be heard.

Imposter syndrome grew into self-doubt, and my thoughts

snowballed from *You aren't good enough to write this essay* to *You aren't good enough to write* any *essay*. I was shame-spiraling, people-pleasing, and, most worrisome, when I wrote, I was performing for the white gaze and consumerism. Thinking of all the ways I would or could be applauded and praised for work I had yet to even complete. True to exactly what I research, fear, doubt, and cynicism were hindering my ability to be present. I had to tune out everything and every voice around me and remind myself that this work, like all my work, was a try. It was, and I am, allowed to be and become without expectation.

My practice of surrendering is one I began to actively work on after I was sexually assaulted during graduate school in 2015. Having been trained as a therapist and four years into my leadership doctoral program, I knew I needed to ask for help immediately but truly lacked the capacity to understand what my healing journey would look like. None of my training or knowledge eased the tightness in my chest or the tension in my jaw; it did not quell my night terrors or ebb the desire to pull my hair out. After three months of flashbacks, panic attacks, barely eating, and irritability I exploded to my therapist, sobbing, asking him why I couldn't seem to shake it, frustrated that I was not proving to be the exception. He said to me, "Stop yelling over it and listen to it: What is your anxiety trying to tell you?" I had never considered that my anxiety was a voice. It would be years until I could recognize that voice as my own, but from that session, I began working on trying to hear my anxiety before it started to scream, when it was still communicating at a whisper. I found that the only way to really hear was to get still and listen; the only way to get through my panic was to surrender.

DURING THE BITTER WORK of healing from my sexual assault, I was able to address a lot of personal trauma. At first, I wanted to categorize "the work" as forgiving myself for not living up to the expectations of being an Educated Black Woman who could handle anything thrown at her and keep her cool. But truly, it was unlearning those expectations and accepting myself for who I am, as I am, that was my salvation. Audre Lorde said, "If I didn't define myself for myself, I would be crunched into other people's fantasies for me and eaten alive." In the time directly after my assault, that sentiment resonated so deeply it became something of a mission statement. It was as if my anxiety was screaming "No!" over and over again at the world, asserting that I would not be crushed under the weight of a narrative I never chose. After my assault, I found myself opting out of performing femininity. I cut all my hair off. I stopped wearing perfume and makeup. I all but abandoned my love of fashion. I was less available; I no longer had the capacity for caretaking and nurturing that I had before. I became much more selfish and self-centered. I felt the pull from some around me to "get over it" or to "at least not talk about it so much," when my inclination was to lean into my pain and speak openly about it. I wanted to be allowed to be a mess and in repair. So, from the day after it happened, I kept a public blog and wrote, sometimes multiple times a day. I was finding my strength in ways that were foreign to me previously because

I was listening to my own voice instead of the echoes of expectation. I learned that being an Educated Black Woman
meant asking for help a lot, but most of all it required me to
completely redefine the idea of strength. In fact, I took the
opportunity to begin to redefine a lot of things.

On a trip to Santa Fe to visit a former professor of mine,
Rose, I sat in the parking lot of a grocery store and sobbed,
telling her how I did not know if I could make it through the
doctoral program. At the time, I felt not only overwhelmed
by my PTSD, but completely uprooted. I genuinely felt as
though I was losing my mind, and as someone who had been
outperforming even my own expectations in graduate school
before my assault, I was panicked as I saw it all slipping
away. I could no longer juggle teaching and research and
work. I could no longer be a social butterfly, attending happy
hours and networking events, volunteering for various community service organizations. I was constantly tired. I was
irritable, often volatile. I felt like a time bomb, never knowing when a panic attack was going to come on so strong it
would leave me unable to get up off the floor for the rest of
the day. I told Rose every fear I had for my career and my
ability to rise to the occasion of my research, which was set
to be deeply complex and personal. In this moment, I was
truly emotionally bare with Rose, and her response was to
tell me something that would stay with me for many days to
come, including today. She told me:

> Environmental factors matter a great deal in the rip-
> ening of grapes. If, for example, a grape does not get
> enough sunlight or gets too much light or warmth

from the sun, it can cause the fruit to go into "survival mode." Sometimes the effect is that grapes do not fully mature and balance sweetness with acidity, and they can be too much of one or the other. So the product is much more concentrated. Similarly, as our environmental factors around us grow extreme, we, too, go into survival mode. This can greatly influence our ability to balance and can cause a sort of concentration of our own product. Jessica, right now you may not be able to produce a full-bodied Cabernet. Right now, you may be a port, and that is okay, isn't it? In fact, it's wonderful. Allow yourself this moment.

The idea that even when the world around me is chaotic, I could still produce and be essential and someone of value was a huge reframe for me. I would cling to the idea that beauty could be derived from pain in true alchemic form even before I could find the strength to live into the message.

I was just back from anxiety- and PTSD-induced disability leave on November 9, 2016, when I learned that in this country sexual violence and misogyny are not a deal breaker for many people. It felt like being assaulted all over again. *I can hurt you and get away with it*. They were the words that Michelle Obama used in her audiobook of *Becoming* that so perfectly described what I felt as I watched men escape accountability, from my own perpetrator to the nation's president. I cried for hours, unable to console myself; I played those words on a loop in my mind because they were exactly what had been echoing in my nightmares for months. *I can hurt you and get away with it.* The horrific sentiment had been the reality of my assault and would continue to be as I moved through the world and a culture that had proved itself, once again, to not value an identity that I could not hide. How could I find my own value and my own worth in a world so determined to convince me of my disposability?

In order to heal and reconcile who I was after feeling such layered violations, I had to do deep-rooted unlearning, relearning, and redefining. Sometimes I've had to fight to see myself through uncolonized eyes. I've had to assure myself that I am not broken or discounted because of what happened to me or because others lack the metrics to appraise my value. To be Black in predominantly white spaces for the majority of your days often means affirming yourself or going without affirmation and representation for long stretches at a time. Aggressions like "I don't see color" or assumptions that educational achievement somehow offsets racism and sexism are laughable and offensive. We are intentionally robbed of opportunities to see the spectrum of who we can become. Without an accurate reflection, our world becomes a funhouse mirror of distorted expectations we can never meet. More often than not, the people around me believe that they are doing me a favor by not acknowledging my differences.

In South Africa, a common greeting is *sawa bona,* which translates to "I see you" or "I acknowledge your existence." The response to this greeting is *sikhona,* which means "I am here—when you see me, you bring me into existence." The more I think about it, the more it feels as though in every space I enter, I am waiting for someone to exchange this pleasantry with, not just in word but in intention. And usually, I am met with silence. What I have come to understand, though, is that most people lack the capacity because so many have only been taught to notice whiteness. This white world of higher education was not designed to acknowledge me as I am, to value me and people who look like me. So often the only way I am allowed to be seen there is when I perform and take on the traits of whiteness. I am heard when I speak "articulately" or dress "professionally." I am allowed to exist, but just barely, the open neglect of my authentic being authorized by someone else's poverty of consciousness.

I started to use the same techniques of healing from my assault in reconciling my professional conflicts. Having grace for myself allowed me to be the Black woman and professor who admitted openly to my students that I was struggling with symptoms from anxiety and panic disorders and PTSD, and invited self-care days into the syllabus as excused absences. I made a choice that if I believed in my own work, that authenticity and mutuality are keys to connection, then I had to combat the shame, doubt, and fear that held me hostage. I repeated the words of Brené Brown, echoing Audre Lorde, as though they were a meditation mantra: *Shame is a tool of the oppressor . . . shame is meant to evoke a trauma response . . . shame is meant to produce fear and fight.* I said them to myself as I fought my way through to get and stay present. I was adamant, even before I believed it, that I had nothing to be ashamed of because I did nothing to deserve what happened to me. Further, I was not responsible for other people's beliefs about me. I began to understand what it meant to move from a place where it was well within my own soul, and that was enough.

Even as I began to heal and find acceptance within myself, it did not mean that my environment would always respond in kind. The dissonance my personal wellness journey would bring in toxic professional environments would be cacophonous. I was out sick from anxiety when my former supervisor called and asked me to resign. They claimed it was in our mutual best interests, but I knew it was because I pushed for accommodations for my health and because as a Black woman, no one thought I deserved them. I knew I was being asked to resign because prior to being out sick for my anxiety disorder, I'd met with many Black and Brown students, helping them advocate against racial mistreatment by faculty and administration. I knew it was because I was not "a good soldier," as my supervisor once asked me to be. I had dared to define myself as something else.

In a conversation with my uncle that will forever stick with me, I was explaining that I did not understand why I could not do what I'd seen others do and just press on, or at the very least shut up more. After losing my job, I did not feel smart, or capable, or like I could ever get back to a place where I could be proud of myself again. My uncle told me, in so many words, this is exactly what you are supposed to be doing. He assured me that not everybody knows how to stand up for themselves, and sometimes when you draw boundaries, not everyone will like them or even agree to them, but you cannot make that your problem. God sent you on assignment here to be you. Don't let anybody else give you another assignment.

I had to figure out how to manage the boundary of being authentic with an environment that did not always welcome variant truths. People do not like to be made to feel uncomfortable. Further, in American society, we go out of our way to avoid discomfort because we have little to no tolerance for experiencing pain. We constantly look for ways to self-soothe, self-medicate, or willfully remain ignorant to pain so that we do not have to introduce suffering to our awareness. We eat comfort foods, we drink to take the edge off, we pay entertainers millions of dollars to provide us with mini respites from our own misery. So when I consider the hesitancy of others to ingest the reality of a Black woman—a fat, dark-skinned, Queer Black woman with mental health disabilities, to be exact—I am not surprised there is no space or tolerance for my story. Do you know what "the problem that has no name" that Betty Friedan spoke of is for a Black woman? It is a primal scream in the middle of a garden party full of white people claiming to *love* that song. We have been singing our pain, painting our truth, dancing our joy, healing and nursing generations, and still people act as though our plight is a mystery, or at best a subplot, and not a symptom of the bitter internal work we all collectively avoid.

As I healed and redefined, I also had to learn how to cultivate new communities and environments that allowed me to be seen and heard for who I was and not just who someone needed me to be. I took a class called The Tao of Heal-

ing, and in it, we got to interview a group of survivalists—
people who habitually prepare for the end for the world.
They spoke about how they planned, what they anticipated,
and why they felt it important to be mindful of the myriad
outcomes for the future. I cannot remember who asked the
question, but from the class came an inquiry that shifted the
way I considered not only the unknown but also working
through spaces from a place of vulnerability and uncertainty. "As a survivalist, someone who is always preparing
for the end of the world and training in how to survive unexpected outcomes, what do you need? Is it a tool? Is it water?
Is it the perfect shelter? What would be the one thing, if you
could think of it, that someone needs to survive the unknown?" The survivalists barely hesitated before asserting,
quite frankly, "The thing you cannot do without is people
you can trust."

I cling to this wisdom more tightly than ever as I watch
the world grow more and more uncertain, with nothing but
unprecedented times ahead. I think to myself, I could lose
everything all over again: my job, my home, people I love.
None of it is promised, and all of it feels particularly temporary right now. Yet because of the mirrors, the people around
me who constantly work to remind me not only of who I am
but that I am this sacred, reverent being, I have found myself resilient in the face of resistance.

I continue to turn over the irony of being proud of my
professional accomplishments and being complicit in a system of classism, exclusion, discrimination, and oppression.
Being successful in higher education was and is very con-
flicting for me, because in order to achieve, you have to be-

come adept at assimilating; and despite your best efforts, you begin to internalize a culture of beliefs you never wanted or asked for in the first place. It is a sacrifice that you don't even realize you're making until you've made it. I find my peace in knowing that my presence within the academy changes the academy. I found myself determined not only to discover and lean into more of who I was as a Black woman, but to do so without shame and in open search of a community that would bring me into existence so long as I committed to being seen.

Maybe you should teach people how to be uncomfortable. It was a thought that my dissertation chair once uttered to me during a meeting, and it has been ringing even louder as of late. At the time, it seemed like an utterly impossible task. How was I going to teach people how to be uncomfortable? Why would anyone trust me to do that? Now I can see that being a Black woman in my professional spaces is a leadership lab model for how to be uncomfortable. Surrender allowed me to stop fighting and listen; and listening allowed me the space I needed to hear the story being told and change it if I dared to. Having a strong community gave me the strength to continue speaking my truth and, working together, I could continue to face any unknown. It was never about what I had to obtain and always about recognizing what I carried innately. Dangerous is the woman who can give herself what she used to seek from others. Limitless is the woman who dares to name herself. The way I see it, shame cannot oppress what acceptance has already claimed for sovereignty.

STEPS TO BEING WHOLE, ON YOUR TERMS

—

AIKO D. BETHEA

Y ES, I WAS THE ONLY ONE ON THIS BIG-ASSED CHEESE *wagon sent once a week to the "white school" for a gifted program. It had to be only about twenty minutes from my school, but it was a different world. Shinier, cleaner. It's where I learned not only that I was poor, but about Black in relation to whiteness. I already knew I was Black, but it's something altogether different to be Black "in relation to whiteness." Having a Japanese mother did nothing to disrupt how the world showed up for me, and how I showed up in the world—Black and poor.*

"What will she eat?" There was a hushed conversation taking place among a few teachers and an administrator. I later realized that this school didn't have the free meal program. It wasn't a Title I school. They were trying to figure out what I would eat for lunch. The other kids had these cool lunch boxes, with Capri Suns, Fruit Roll-Ups—all of the "pricey" snack items that my mother never bought. We had to keep the lights on.

It was embarrassing. No, it was shame. I wanted to hide. Why was I even there? The way I spoke was wrong. My too-small clothes seemed to illuminate and yell, "Look at me!" My hair—just everything about me was wrong. Being Black here was wrong. Being poor here was wrong. I didn't belong.

To be Black and a woman is to be drafted into targeted identity groups that often conflate classism, sexism, racism, genderism. This begins so early when you're "the Only": the only Black child at a predominantly white school, the only Black child in a neighborhood, the only Black child on a sports team, on a street, in a store.

You may become a wealthy and highly educated Black woman, but still, when you're seen, you're seen as everything that a white supremacist society associates with being a Black woman: poor, uneducated, promiscuous, unattractive, sassy, loud. You walk into every room at a deficit. Unacceptable. Unaccepted.

When we're deemed unacceptable, our responses generally fall into four familiar patterns: (1) assimilate, striving for acceptance; (2) fight fire with fire, beating off rejection and judgment first and fighting shame with shame; (3) hide under the radar, invisible and unnoticed; or (4) live wholeheartedly, recognizing white supremacy and deliberately making decisions that honor our values while leaning in to connection, compassion, and courage. The first three options require us to armor up. Brené Brown defines our armor as the thoughts, emotions, and behaviors we apply to protect ourselves, particularly against feelings of uncertainty and vulnerability. Let's dive deeper into each.

1. ASSIMILATING AND STRIVING FOR ACCEPTANCE

When we strive to be accepted—when we seek to appease the system—we often use tools of white supremacy as our armor to gird ourselves against the shame imposed by white supremacy. This armor may help us to feel less vulnerable, less susceptible to attack, and more likely to be deemed acceptable and worthy. This armor affirms that we as Black women "know how to behave" and "are not like the others." The more successful you are in assimilating, the more exceptional you are. You're less "Black" and more "white." Acceptable. Worthy. Some examples of this type of armor:

- **Academic credentials:** measured by the level of education completed and the elitism of schools attended
- **Professional titles:** working at a respected employer or having an elevated role or title (e.g., manager, lawyer, doctor)
- **Marital status:** evidence that you are chaste and respectable, that someone wants you and feels you are worthy to be married (bonus if your husband has a job with stature)
- **Beauty that mimics white features:** a fair, light complexion; hair set straight, or "mixed-girl curly," not kinky; a petite physique
- **Money and material items:** not necessarily the same as financial security, but a display of luxury goods
- **Pedigree:** parental or family stature and legacy

2. FIGHTING FIRE WITH FIRE

When we react to white supremacist culture, we may literally curse it and give it the finger. This may look like throwing all of the respectability politics aside, being seen, and being heard. In this instance, the reasoning may be more about "to hell with white people and to hell with what anyone thinks about me. I'll wear what you deem unacceptable, say what I want how I want whenever I want—and I'm not hustling to be approved by white standards." We move against shame and may even fight shame with shame.

The armor may be toughness and nonconformity. "I'm not giving you a chance to reject me because I'm not even trying to be accepted by you. I reject you and all of your expectations before you reject or try to shame me." Here, the motive for being nonconformist and wielding a tough veneer is to cast off shame with anger and defiance. The goal is to cut off expectations of acceptance and connection by intentionally disconnecting and mitigating the feeling of exclusion and being judged.

3. HIDING UNDER THE RADAR

This looks like playing small, not using your voice, avoiding any shine or attention. "If I just lie low and mind my business, no one will have anything to say." With this approach, we keep ourselves hidden and quiet. We hide our successes, as they can often make us a target. Many times Black people are even told, "Never let them see what you have. The last

thing a white person wants to see is a Black person with anything better than they have." We're not supposed to win.
We're not supposed to be successful. We're not supposed to
be ambitious. And we certainly are not supposed to have
more success than white people. Because of this mandate,
we use the shame shield of moving away. As with assimila-
tion and fighting fire with fire, this approach fosters discon-
nect. Furthermore, we never realize our own strength,
abilities, and worth.

*WHEN I SEPARATED (VERY amicably) and moved out of the
family house, I had to secure a new place that would ac-
commodate me and my boys. This meant I had to identify
as a single Black mother. In Seattle, every landlord or
rental agent was white. I was asked if my kids were loud, if
there were any custody issues or a restraining order. There
was an obvious narrative that these white folx told themselves about me. I was asked again and again about my
employer and position. It was like they expected me to
switch my story and be caught in a lie. Note that all this
information was clear in my rental application: attorney,
six-figure salary, leader at the Bill & Melinda Gates Foundation. I always brought a copy of my credit report that
reflected a credit score categorized as "excellent." And yet,
because of this constant shaming and humiliating experience, I gave up on attempting to rent a home and just
rented a standard commercial apartment.*

Shame is often the barrier to wholehearted living. It can

confine us on a hamster wheel, always racing for approval and acceptance, hiding our presence, or sapping our energy in efforts to be armored. When we share our stories, practice empathy, and deconstruct the beliefs that induce shame, we become "shame resilient." Shame resilience provides the gift of wholehearted living. An extra bonus of shame resilience: dismantling white supremacy. Here are some tools of shame resilience:

- **Deconstruction and naming:** Social justice scholars provide language and frameworks that deconstruct white supremacy, patriarchy, transphobia, and other systems of inequity. Standards of intellect, womanhood, and beauty were never inclusive of Black women. Reading the words of Audre Lorde, Kimberlé Crenshaw, Paula Giddings, James Baldwin, bell hooks, Sonya Renee Taylor, Ibram X. Kendi, and so many other Black intellectuals provides visibility, affirmation, and historical facts that are rarely taught. Breaking down power and privilege by acquiring language and recognizing shared narratives enables us to see and name inequity and shame.
- **Community and connection:** Black women have held one another's pain forever. We have formed connections with the flicker of an eye, a knowing nod, a warm hug, and a slight hand gesture. No words spoken. When we choose to tell our stories and stand in our values, we disempower white supremacy. We expose injustice, we validate our presence, we affirm our existence.

The power of a community that sees us and validates our experience is invaluable. My Sister Circle—my community of Black women who see me, hear me, and hold me—is my source of infinite empathy, truth-telling, and protection. We encounter the same system that excludes us. We know the shame-inducing narratives. Through it all we hold one another and share tears and joy, wins and losses. This Sister Circle that I have is not the first of its kind. It has existed among Black women since the beginning—before white supremacy. It is the love that allows us to thrive despite misogyny, classism, transphobia, and all of the systems that work to annihilate us.

- **Creatives and possibility:** J. California Cooper, Octavia Butler, Dorothy Height, adrienne maree brown, Jordan Peele, Anita Baker, Cheo Hodari Coker, Langston Hughes, Sonia Sanchez, Ta-Nehisi Coates, Jason Reynolds, Lena Waithe, Ava DuVernay, Frank Ocean, Beyoncé—our creatives who bring lyrics and rhythm, images and characters, and futures that validate us—create spaces where we thrive, and dreams for us to keep dreaming. They provide us spaces to breathe freely that are in this world and beyond this world. Every human spirit needs connection and hope.

- **Spirituality and purpose:** There's a space between legacy and ancestry that anchors our existence. Some call it our higher calling, and others refer to it as our higher purpose. It's where we believe and know that despite the systems and hardships, we have a purpose that supersedes the here and now. We recognize that our very existence transcends and defies what we see, are taught, and experience daily.

DID I EVER SMILE? Rarely. Instead, I had a perpetual chip on my shoulder. I remember being at a New Year's Eve party and a white girl accidentally shoved me. I lost it. My brother and my cousin who was visiting from out of town had to pull me off the girl. I believe I was pretty much going for blood. It was like the straw that broke the camel's back. In college, this was the case as well. I often found myself just being angry. Angry all the time. At Smith College, in a sea of whiteness telling me how wrong I was, sometimes it was overt, but usually it was a thousand (micro)aggressions a minute. To deal, I had to fly under the radar or sometimes default to "I don't give a damn" or "Get the fuck out of my way."

We are vulnerable even when we are not. We are vulnerable even when we have not chosen to be. The existence of Black women is always under assault. Our hair is an insult and our bodies are violated. Our Black brothers, sons, fathers, daughters, mothers, sisters, grandmothers, aunties are all vulnerable. We can disappear, be assaulted, be murdered under the color of law without recourse. Despite our credentials and accolades, we can be the first to be laid off. We know this and we are reminded of this. We are always vulnerable—living without certainty and at risk.

But *to choose to be vulnerable,* as in emotionally exposed, that is something we have control over. When and to whom will we show our emotions? We get to choose this.

We may expose that we didn't come from a two-parent household, our hair fresh out of braids, or without the perm or wrap; speak in free-flowing colloquial; share our stories and our experiences of fear, joy, grief, and shame; bare our tears and celebrate our wins with our uninhibited laughter. When we are willing to discard armor, we are free, and we free others.

Among one another we may opt to be vulnerable for several reasons. We may simply trust our shared language and journey. Or we may be vulnerable in a moment when our pain is too great to bear. I have yet to meet another sister who has not had this moment—the moment you are so numbed, until another sister, another brown-skinned girl, hugs you fiercely and gently. Then the tears and the sobs come. You may not even know her name, but you know each other. You see each other and you feel each other's pain.

Place and space matter. Being vulnerable in places and spaces where we are "not supposed to be," or where our truth has never been spoken and our vulnerability has never been seen, is powerful. Being seen and compelling others to witness the violence of white supremacy invites accountability. It injects truth into a facade. This truth-telling is a powerful step in dismantling white supremacy, putting cracks in it. White women and anyone else with a targeted identity reap the benefits of Black women's willingness to be vulnerable. When we are vulnerable we are literally breaking chains. In the moments when we are vulnerable in these white spaces through our truth-telling, we're extending an invitation to authenticity and potential connection to those who aren't assaulted by white supremacy in the same way as Black women.

We may not be able to control the fact that we are by default vulnerable in this society—in this world—but we can share our narrative on our terms and use it for connection and empowerment instead of hustling for our worth.

"IT WAS AMAZING TO go back to Israel to trace my family's lineage all the way to the home my great-grandparents lived in. And then, to see my family listed in the Book of Names!" This was the conversation at a work dinner. We were all women on a shared leadership team and I was the only person of color. Two of my colleagues were Jewish and shared this pretty amazing history. The other two colleagues began to talk about their families' stories of origin and immigration. I was quiet. Is this where I say that I don't know my lineage, because, well, you know, the "S" word? Then I'm left with a few options. None are mutually exclusive: (a) be the joy wrecker, (b) manage their guilt and awkwardness throughout the meal, or (c) shrug off their defensiveness and disdain. Note that each of these options leaves me even more ostracized and as the one who isn't a "good team player." So I order another drink and put on my face of immersed interest.

When considering what it takes to get to vulnerability with white people, this differs for each individual. Based on my experience and what has been shared with me, there are themes for when we can trust and venture to be vulnerable.

- **Learner mindset:** Engaging with someone who is invested in actively learning for the sake of growing and improving can further relationships with white people. Note that there is a difference between embracing learning for the purpose of establishing a deeper connection and creating positive change, and learning simply to know or to satisfy penchants for voyeurism. We have little desire to be someone's teacher for free or a project topic they are learning about. Evidence of a learner mindset includes active listening, embracing getting something wrong instead of being defensive, and inviting accountability.

- **Acknowledgment of privilege and inequity:** White people who understand and own their privilege and the inequity it can yield are easier to be vulnerable with. This should translate into greater self-awareness and therefore showing up differently. Showing up differently includes the white person not exercising power and privilege over us and recognizing impact over intention.

- **Bravery:** We cannot conclude because a white person is an active learner who acknowledges their privilege and recognizes inequity that they will also be brave enough to take action or use their voice to counter inequity. Seeing a white person who is a learner, who is actively using their status, privilege, and knowledge to be present and vocal in countering inequity, is powerful. These are the people I want in my corner, and they're likely the only white people you will see at my kitchen table. Yes, I know that the trapdoor of racism is ever-present in relationships with white people. Their blind spots will show up. Even if it is not their doing, it can be their family members and other white friends who send you spiraling by pulling that trapdoor of racism open on you. Your expectation is that the white friend or peer will swiftly deal with the situation—even if you have to call their attention to it.

AFTER I STUDIED BLACK women and was immersed in our history and our stories, I saw me. Like, I just saw me. I didn't see me through the lens of whiteness and the stories that are told about me and people who look like me. I saw me. I saw what I am capable of. I saw that my story started at a deficit because I was reading a narrative written by someone who created a version of me that was twisted and wrong.

Seeing more Black women calling out (not calling in) white supremacy when they see it is empowering for all of us. We see this on all platforms of social media now. Sisters are out here saying their piece and not being shy about saying, "I'm speaking." Even if this white supremacist society never agrees to see us on our own terms, we're creating our own spaces. Pulling up a chair to a table setting of white supremacy? No thanks.

TO YOU: VULNERABLE MOTHER

A Choreo-Essay

—

IMANI PERRY

> My life seems to be an increasing revelation of the inti-
> mate face of universal struggle. You begin with your fam-
> ily and the kids on the block, and next you open your eyes
> to what you call your people and that leads you into land
> reform into Black English into Angola leads you back to
> your own bed where you lie by yourself, wondering if you
> deserve to be peaceful, or trusted or desired or left to the
> freedom of your own unfaltering heart. And the scale
> shrinks to the size of a skull: your own interior cage.
>
> —**JUNE JORDAN,**
> *Some of Us Did Not Die:*
> *New and Selected Essays*

WHEN DID YOU BEGIN TO AWAKEN WITH A SWOL-
len face? I mean the one that is not the result of a cold or
hours of weeping. The one that is your earned face. Worry
makes its mark. If not there, in the steady ache between
your shoulder blades, a steady headache, the corn worried

to red on white atop your right third toe. You sigh unexpect-
edly and often.

I started this piece with June Jordan, a habit of mine, because she grants me remarkable confidence, and because she
could tell a world in a paragraph. The intimate face of the
universal struggle blooms when we come of age. We all love,
hopefully hard—the kind of love that cannot be destroyed.
We fear death. We hate heartbreak. We work too hard and
rest too infrequently. Those are near-universal things. But it
can get more challenging still. Some terms are harder to live
with. According to identity, responsibility, and experience,
the universal struggle sometimes has a starker, and harsher,
expression. I know that June Jordan was talking to me, a
Black woman, worrying about her family and kids and the
kids on the block and the people and the prisons.

Sometimes, I have read, people use the second person
instead of "I" when they are talking about something that is
especially painful because it is less frightening if you distance yourself from it. Perhaps that's what I just did. But I
hope that it also works as a way to reach across from me to
you, reader. I hope that in the way that the epigraph above
hit me, rang loudly inside my head when I read the words,
that when you read "you" you saw you, and me, maybe a you
and me that both of us find difficult to face and even harder
to forget.

VULNERABLE PEOPLE, I HAVE read, are defined by being
susceptible to physical or emotional attack or injury. If you

are a person whose very body marks you as deserving of disregard, or as available for violence, you are vulnerable no matter how strong or smart you are. And so I wonder: Why don't we always call being Black in the United States being vulnerable? It is inarguably so.

I am a Black mother. And if you are like me, you may have played with doll babies for long hours as a child. You tended them with care. You rocked or "shaked" the baby, gently soothing in the way you saw your own caretakers do. Sometimes you fussed at your children but then you picked them up and kissed their plastic cheeks. You sewed dresses with big uneven stitches and regretted cutting off their waxy curls. You never once doubted that your attentiveness and sweet love was more than enough for your babies. Your confidence was remarkable.

But you had to grow up. We grew up. And as we grew up and became real mothers, so much was eked away that we grew with each season of life more aware of the precarity of our task. Black mothers' vulnerability is particular. And inside that specific reality, that ambiguous word "vulnerable" collides against itself. Because vulnerable also means that you are subject to higher penalties for every misdeed, every failure. But also, vulnerable means that you need special care and protection because you are susceptible to physical or emotional attack or injury. Here is the tension: If I reveal my anguish, my human errors are exposed, judged, evaluated, and punished. With little hope for sensitivity. Empathy, writ large, is reserved for other types of people, less vulnerable ones. Empathy is often shaped by white supremacy. It glides over us, rarely resting long enough to witness our humanness.

I'll tell you a few stories to make things clearer.

Once upon a time there was a mother and a child. The mother read stories to her son each night. She gave him plenty of hugs and warm baths. She joined the PTA when he began school. It was that year that his breathing became labored, strained, terrifyingly vulnerable. The big stone schoolhouse was a sick building. Poison radiated from it, because who cares much about schools for children like him? And she would run from work every time he struggled. And she missed work, and was punished, then fired, for tardiness and absences; and he missed school and faced the consequence for tardiness and absences. And when they weren't around, the people talked about what a shame it was that neither fulfilled their promise. And soon there were so many things to worry about that the nighttime stories had no magic and were set aside. And the hugs grew rare, feeling desperate rather than sweet.

Once upon a time there was a mother and a child. The mother had scaled every professional height. She kept things precise; excellence was her brand and promotion. The daughter was smart and gregarious and the apple of her mother's eye. But "too much" for a Black girl in the eyes of many. Pricks of envy turned to sniping. The girl grew embarrassed. How could she tell her mother, so precise, how much she was failing at staying in her place? Loneliness stuck in her craw. Ugliness stared back at her from the mirror, in their eyes. Soon her spirit was cracked. The mother watched, castigated, encouraged, implored until she too began to see failure in the mirror. The one thing that mattered most was her greatest inadequacy: motherhood.

Once upon a time there was a mother who slipped away in mind but not body. There was a child who tried to mother her. The child cooked. The child cleaned. The child adored. The mother, having been hungry her whole life, ate at the child's life, grateful but selfish. The child, hungry her whole life, looked for someone, anyone, to hear their loneliest of songs. You can find them now, swimming upstream against the tide of neglect, with hope waning, but hoping still.

Maybe you felt the stories. Or you've heard their melodies. Caged birds sing the most beautiful songs. Paul Laurence Dunbar told us so. But they also pace and peck. Watch them: Sometimes their habits look frenetic. Sometimes they are so still you wonder, *Do animals get bored?*

Or, *Is that bird still alive?* A jolt and they startle. Like you do when you have a terrible flashback.

Some might think the caged bird sings because it has the gift of transcendence.

Or simply because it is beautiful.

Grace is a truer word.

Grace is not, however, enough, even when it has to be enough. I mean, really, we can praise it all we want.

But will somebody, anybody, open the door?

Inside my own interior cage, the one June Jordan told me about, I peer at my swollen face. I feel around for my heart. Underneath the racing it often aches. There is so much to be concerned with, so much beyond control, so much that is worrisome, so much that cannot be changed. Vulnerable parents raise vulnerable children. Children who step out from under our embrace and face the slings and arrows without us. They are pierced. They have watched us and learned to cleverly cover over wounds, to laugh or lash at them, because vulnerable means subject to higher penalties or deserving of disregard. "Weak" is something we curl up our lips at. What a terrible thing to do when nurture is the appropriate response. And what a lesson to our young. If they learn that lesson too well, we teach them how not to ask when they need help, and therefore we cannot give them the special care and protection they need and deserve, because they too are vulnerable masquerading as invulnerable. What a cruel choreography.

The sociologists and social critics, not all but many, will tell you about cycles that must be broken. They mean the sociological things like poverty, prison, employment, disease, premature birth and death, violence, and homelessness. And they will tell you that breaking the cycle is our duty, especially the duty of mothers. And they never flinch or hesitate or let their mouths tremble before the ugliness spilling out of them. They never ask themselves: *How is it that I keep telling the vulnerable to not be vulnerable? How is it that I fasten my eyes to write down even more judgment on top of judgment, and will not acknowledge the mounds on her back that threaten to bury her?*

Even seeds need water. And air that can be reached.

The sharply worded assessment is written again and again: Black women have too much (more than anyone else) cancer, heart disease, and diabetes. Black women have strokes, chlamydia, syphilis, HIV, and hypertension. They give birth to babies who weigh too little and die too frequently more than anyone else.

The data say we die more than other women from the worst of these.

The data say we, and our children, carry too much flesh and too much fat.

I hate these statistics.

I hate that they're real evidence.

But what I hate even more is that they are so often presented without context. And by context I mean the culture and values that shape our lives. They are, in fact, secondary details to a primary truth about the world and the way it treats us. I would like another set of facts. I would like a visual constellation of the thousands of stressors electrifying our brains each day. I would like a map of the mundane experience of defeat in love, in work, in housing, in caretaking. I would like a list of obstacles before us. I would like someone to draw us standing before the mountain barefoot, slue-footed and sleep-deprived, expected to climb. I want a more honest rendering. I want gentle eyes. That is a first step.

I have no pep talk to offer because such words only crush you when they falter. *You can do it!* Right before you couldn't. I have felt the crush myself. Instead, my words, to myself and to us, to you, are tenderness, warning, and warming. You simply cannot be kind to yourself and also accept the structure and judgment of a racist and sexist society. These days you hear a lot of talk about self-care. I'm telling you that there is an indispensable tool, a necessary part of self-care that cannot be left out. The tool is refusing to accept the terms of a world that builds you into it as vulnerable. And that goes for parenting and protecting as well. We can bemoan what we don't have, we can and should decry what is unfair and what hurts, but the moment we turn on ourselves, we have chosen cruelty over love.

As we prepare our children for this world, our challenging task sits at the crossroads of a vulnerability that we ourselves never get to stop managing. We know the risks of sharing our tears, of admitting weakness. We also know, or ought to know, that if we prepare our children with that lesson we are teaching them to beat their chests when weeping is more appropriate, to swallow fear when screaming is necessary. And even if we never say it, our examples can be violent. Letting them be fully human can be scary, but it is necessary. Letting ourselves be fully human feels like it's against the rules. I kindly say in response: Fuck the rules, be free.

I think, and I say "think" because I will not pretend to know a world that doesn't yet exist, that the lesson we have to teach ourselves is how to do caretaking without denying our vulnerability and even our weaknesses and fallibility. This is what I take Jordan to mean when she speaks of revelation. We have to be naked with our failures and shame and ask our loved ones to help us stand up and grow through them. And this task is probably hardest when it comes to our children's vulnerability. It tears at us. If you've ever seen a mother lash out at a child, you've probably seen a mother who is convulsing with self-loathing over having to stand before her child inadequate. You've probably seen a mother who has chosen to wound rather than be naked because she thinks that is what the child needs. If you've seen a mother layering thick guilt onto her child's spirit, I think you've probably seen a mother who is terrified that her failure has cost her the greatest love of her life: the one from her child.

If that mother is you, you're not alone.

If that mother sees you seeing her, show her another way.

Build something else, with her.

Easier said than done. Anyone who has been through therapy knows that feeling at the end of the fifty minutes when your life stands in tatters, spread out everywhere, and you are charged with walking out and back into regular life. It is terrifying. As much as the discipline of therapeutic practice has its virtues, the vulnerability of exposure is real. We need more than the fifty minutes. We also need daily ritual. We need held hands. We need common purpose. We need a cloud of loving witnesses. For you, for your babies, for me, for mine. Someone must share not only the burden but also the climb. You know how it says in the Bible "where two or more are gathered"? I do not believe that that is a statement that is solely or even primarily about church. I believe it is about the essential spiritual requirement of community.

When you stand in community, you begin with a basic question: *Who am I?* That's as fraught and dangerous a task as anything else for a vulnerable woman. Can you define yourself in ways that have little if anything to do with how you're placed in society, but everything to do with what you like, who you love, what makes you laugh, what rocks your spirit, what leaves you satisfied? Can you notice your feelings without judgment? Can you use them just as information without layering on evaluation? Can you think about the things that make you and your loved ones, especially your children, beautiful, sweet, joyful, without putting them in comparison to others? Can you decide this all matters? Can we? Please. Together.

In this task you let go. You let go of the trivial things that you believe offer you an advantage in this world, and of the big things that threaten to swallow you up. Those sizes are not my judgment but our doing. I didn't make up the habits. I'm just calling it how I see it. Risky business, I know, but there's risk in every virtue. Let's risk together. This is what Tarana Burke, my friend and our editor, taught me. That the way to risk enough to share that intimate face of universal truth is to risk together.

Where two or more are gathered, the moments of plaintive moaning are backed by a melody. Breaks in the tune are what we call, in Black music, "worrying the line." Worrying the line is a phrase for when the expected tune is disrupted. Sometimes the worrying break is a holler, sometimes it's a shout, sometimes it reaches toward the sky, and sometimes it is heavy and full-bodied. June Jordan said that there are two ways to worry words: "One is hoping for the greatest possible beauty in what is created. The other is to tell the truth."

I choose to give over my worrying to this kind, this kind that we need. Not a vanity and not a judgment. If you shout, I plan to come running, and not alone. I plan to pry apart the gates of that interior cage and grab you up into an embrace. Me too. For me too.

WHERE THE TRUTH RESTS

—

TARANA BURKE

D EAR TARANA,

Take a breath, dear heart. I know you. I don't want you to overwhelm yourself with what I am about to say—so I want you to stop, *breathe,* and relax, and keep coming back to this whenever you need to as we move forward.

Agreed? Good.

It has become increasingly popular to pen letters to our younger selves as a means of healing old wounds and prompting empathy and forgiveness for ourselves that we perhaps couldn't muster at the onset of our trauma. I've employed this practice myself in my work over the years, but I am going to take a chance and go in a different direction this time by writing to us in the future. I don't know when exactly. This may just be a salve one day when we need it more than any previous day, or it may be a routine elixir that we pull out often to beat back that all-consuming tidal wave that makes us feel diseased. These are our words to use how we see fit.

We are sick.

I just need to get this out first, because I know how it makes you feel to hear it or read it. You will want to buck at this characterization, or dissect and explain, but I need you to sit with it for a moment. No one is here but us. No one can hear you. No one is judging you. That word "sick" alone won't kill you. But you have to know in this moment as I am sending you these words, we are in danger of spilling out of the container that we have spent so much time carefully building for ourselves.

Remember when we first started?

Oh, we thought we were so clever, didn't we? And we were, to some extent. We were right that no one wanted to hold the weight of what we were carrying in our little first-grade hands. They wanted a good girl. And a smart girl. So we gave them what they wanted and put those heavy things like fear and shame and confusion in our small box so that we could take it out when no one was looking. It was brilliant, until the box started getting full and then got too heavy. And so we started to build new ones. This is where the sickness started, beloved. I know our memory sometimes won't carry us back that far, but you have to know that is because we refused to step into the container with both feet. Recently, though, I've had to—for both of our sakes.

As soon as I entered, boxes started falling off the shelves into my hands. Remember that sleepover? There weren't many in our childhood. We were seven and it was probably summertime. We begged Mommy to let us spend the night with our neighbor and her daughter, who was our best friend at the time. As we were going to bed, our friend's daddy asked us for a good-night kiss. We knew him well, but the pee still shot into our bladder, beating hard against our little pelvis. Our breathing got uneven and our heart was racing. Instead of running into his open arms, we ran into the bathroom, almost missing the toilet bowl from trying to get our pajama pants off so fast.

When we were done, we just sat there with our legs dangling over the commode, letting the cold press deep into our calves so that we wouldn't fall over from the toilet seat. We felt a rush of things that we didn't like. Some we knew already, like the shame and fear, and others were new, like the anxiousness and embarrassment, but all of it went into the container. Remember how our stomach turned when our neighbor knocked on the door and then peeked in to see if we were okay? We were very much not okay, but we left the bathroom and forced our little body to run to him and plant a kiss on his cheek anyway. Mommy had to come upstairs and get us that night because we wouldn't stop crying under the covers after we were all tucked in. The adults said we were afraid of sleeping in new places.

We didn't tell them that we were afraid because we were always afraid.

I know we haven't thought of that night in a very long time, but please trust me when I say that having a clear understanding of the roots of this illness will go a long way to helping us manage it well.

By middle school we had become so skilled at expanding the container and carefully, neatly packing our stuff inside that it didn't occur to us that we would have any use for those things, so we stopped pulling them out—even when no one was looking. We so desperately wanted to become what we were pretending to be. Remember how harshly we treated ourselves? In the seventh grade, when we were selected to deliver the liturgy during all-school Mass, we were so excited on the outside and terrified on the inside. We would have to pray and lead the entire school through the call and response. We had never really spoken in public—besides running our mouth in the schoolyard at recess—and now we had allowed our performance of perfection, including that bubbly, outgoing personality, to push us into a real-life performance that we were not ready for. When the time came—even though we had rehearsed, prepped, and done all the things we could to prepare for when we had to show up more closely to authentic—we failed. The memory of standing in that pulpit staring out at everyone in the school, from the restless kindergarten kids to the irritated and then mildly amused eighth-grade kids, and then being able to speak only barely above a whisper, stammering through a prayer we knew backward and forward, followed by an uncontrollable attack of nervous laughter, was a recurring nightmare for so many years. I'm sure remembering that long run from the pulpit down the corridor and out the massive church doors still makes your stomach knot up and the hairs stand up on the back of your neck. That's what is happening to me now. But we have to remember, because what happened at our neighbors' house the night of the sleepover, and in the church that day, and so many times in between and after, was an anxiety attack. I know we are more than familiar with them now, but they didn't start in our twenties, as we had long told ourselves—they just got worse then. Children are resilient, and maybe that's why we were able to mask these attacks most of the time. But children are also porous and soak up all of the messages spoken and unspoken that surround them on a daily basis. At the time, the whispers to keep silent and appear normal were deafening. And so we did.

There is no blame here. We were just trying to survive.

The container started to show signs that it would not always hold up that day in the church. We messed up the liturgy in front of the whole school and were hurt and embarrassed, but our brain had already taught us to turn that into anxiety and shame. That same cycle has repeated over and over so many times in our life that we almost don't know how to function without them. Almost.

I know you recall the first time we heard the word "anxiety" related to our behavior. We were around twenty-two, riding back to Selma from Birmingham with girlfriends. I still don't know where it came from, but out of nowhere one of our "episodes" started. We had come up with that name to describe the tightening in our chest, labored breathing, and dizzy feeling that sometimes snuck up on us. Normally, it was like that movie *The Blob,* where an amorphous, icky feeling slowly took hold of us and wouldn't relent. It sometimes started in our feet and made our legs feel like jelly as it crept up past our knees to our thighs. Other times it attacked from our stomachs and spread both ways like a giant burst. But we were masters. We had gotten so good at removing ourselves from people as soon as the first feeling hit that I bet if we could have watched ourselves, it would have been like seeing a master illusionist at work. That day in the car was different. We had nowhere to go and we couldn't hide, and so we had to feel all of our feelings in front of folks for the first time. One of our girlfriends opened the window to make sure we were getting fresh air while the other put her arm around us and talked us through steadying our breathing. She kept us cradled in her arms until our breathing normalized and the car stopped spinning. When they asked us if we were all right, we said it was just a thing that happens sometimes when we have been in a car for too long, but thankfully our girlfriend knew better. She said very carefully, "I think you had an anxiety attack." She then described what they were and the possible causes, and we nodded and smiled, but even listening to her turn our episodes into a concrete thing with a name was causing us more anxiety. We probably made a joke to brush it off and change the subject. We do that a lot. Do you still do that?

We promised that day that we would talk to our doctor about it. But we didn't. We found space in the container and tucked that episode away with everything else. This pattern went on for far longer than we ever want to admit, Tarana— but you remember what happened when we were forced to pay attention. It was during Hurricane Katrina. We had been working for three days straight setting up the temporary shelter with our folks and trying to locate our family and friends who had gotten caught in the storm down in New Orleans. We would get up in the morning and go to the Red Cross to check in for new people needing lodging, and then go across the river to our community center, which had been transformed into a holding center for donations. We'd work there for a few hours, and then drive twenty-three miles round trip bringing stuff out to the campsite that was now a shelter. We were exhausted. The work itself was keeping us calm, or so we thought, but it was just holding us together. Nothing going on inside of us was calm, because our heart was heavy waiting on news about if our folks had survived or not.

Finally, on the third day, we got a call. In so many ways that call changed our lives. Someone put a cellphone into our hand while screaming and crying out, "It's Uncle Ted!" We grabbed the phone and tried to hold our composure while listening to him rattle off scattered details. The tears were falling hard to the point of blurring our vision. We handed the phone back and attempted to pull ourselves together, but our head was spinning. Before we could make a move, our weight shifted and we grabbed on to the window of the minivan we were leaning on. "Are you okay?" we could hear someone ask. But we were paralyzed, or at least it felt that way. And then, we blacked out. When we came to, we acted awful. People were fussing over us, and we started cussing and screaming for them to get off of us, and we went and sat in the building for a moment. After drinking water and sitting still for maybe ten minutes, we emerged from the building and shot daggers at anyone who asked what happened.

We moved on as if it were nothing, and it was such a busy time that no one followed up or asked any more questions. I wish they would have. I wish someone would have pushed us to explain why we were acting so irrational when people were just offering help. I wish someone could have seen through that hard-as-nails exterior to help us see that we had just experienced something we had never quite felt before.

A tear in the seam.

It was so scary to us, because we were not supposed to be this person. The container was supposed to hold. We were not crazy, we were strong. We never, ever fell apart in public. In fact, we went to great lengths to be even-keeled in most situations. The only emotions we wielded freely were our versions of *happiness* and *anger*. Fear, panic, sadness, vulnerability, and the like were off-limits. We had heard our mother say enough times how she hated when women cried in public to *know better* than to let ourselves get caught in that "weak woman" web. The need to manage the array of emotions that visited us on a regular basis was predicated on our need to be strong—at all times. Strong women are collected. They are sharp and aware and impervious. That moment, at the car, as we recovered and folks were fussing over us, we felt overwhelmed and scared—but more than anything we felt betrayed by our brain. We had done so much work to neatly pack so much stuff away, and in one moment it seemed to have all come undone.

That's where we are today. Undone.

I know you want to know why I am dredging up all of these memories that we worked so hard to keep just out of our periphery, but I have to. I am worried about us. Therapy got us out of the darkest places, and I am grateful for that. The books we read and the people we have talked to have helped us master the language of the healing and healthy, but we know what's true.

Breathe. Let your heart collect itself. We aren't in any danger right now.

What's true is that we still grind our teeth in our sleep three decades after a dentist first told us that it could be a problem. Now it's a problem. We paid handsomely to fix the problem, but how long did we wear the mouth guard? The moment the dentist said it was necessary our first thought was, *I'm not doing that.* We are so stubborn. The first doctor we trusted with a few of our secrets was Dr. Pena, our obstetrician. We were most committed to our mental and physical health when we were pregnant. We told him about all of the manifestations of stress and anxiety in our lives and how they mostly affected our sleep: night terrors, teeth grinding, sleepwalking, talking in our sleep, and of course, insomnia. He is the one who first told us "the body and mind are connected" and suggested a therapist. We stared at the phone number he gave us for a long time until the piece of paper it was on became a grocery list or scratch pad or something.

We made a bold promise that we would prioritize dealing with these issues so that we didn't pass them down to our baby. That didn't happen. Right now we have learned that we have five cavities. After a lifetime of none, we now have a mouthful because we have ground down the ridges that protect the teeth. We have damaged our gums and our jawbone from biting down so hard. We were mortified as the dentist gently explained the condition of our mouth to us and asked, "Are you stressed?"

Are we stressed, still?

We once wrote an essay called "Death to the Strong Black Woman." It was one of our first published pieces, and we were so worried about it that we stayed up until the wee hours of the morning to make edits and more edits. When the editor asked us if we could add another piece about love and relationships, we agreed, though we were already exhausted. We got that second piece done in one night because we were determined to be excellent. I don't know how we missed the connection between strength and excellence. Do you get it now? I know you probably still call yourself a freedom fighter, but I wonder if you have mapped out a path to your own liberation.

Black Excellence.

Strong Black Woman.

Thank a Black Woman.

Black Girl Magic.

They are all about our labor, not our liberation.

We will die on the vine for them if we don't stop and realize that we are sick.

Can we talk about the stroke?

I don't know how long it's been for you, but for me it's been less than a year. Three years into our newfound "celebrity," this seemingly random medical emergency was what finally halted us in our tracks. This was supposed to be our tipping point. It was supposed to be the thing that turned us around. It was our undoing.

That day was no busier than others. Even though we were quarantined in a pandemic, our work had somehow doubled.

We had our usual meetings and Zoom calls and a full agenda, but we were tired—no, exhausted—by midday. It was a different kind of exhaustion, though, extremely low energy and spirits. By early evening we did the thing we always threatened to do—we lay down for a nap. An hour later panic woke us up. Our body felt as though we had been in a fight, and our right side couldn't move. We managed to call out to Kaia, who called our fiancé into the room. But I want to back up for a moment and recall with you the moment right before they entered the room. We were lying still on the bed muffling our cries. Every attempt to lift our right arm or roll to our side failed, and each try made our heart race faster. After the second try, we thought about calling out but instead closed our eyes and attempted to "calm down." It is the method we had been using for years during anxiety attacks and those dizzy spells we had decided were vertigo when no doctor could or would explain them. It wasn't working. The tears were coming faster. And we were scared.

We still didn't call out. We lay there for minutes—what could have been precious minutes—thinking. We had one burning question at the moment: *What will be exposed if I let this play out?*

Then our mind was off to the races.

What if this was low iron?

We thought about how we let our diet go so badly that we had gained at least twenty pounds.

What if it was some major anxiety attack? Would they have to medicate me?

What if it was that secret compulsion I had? Would the world dismiss me as crazy?

What about all the work I had done and still had to do?
What happens to that if I let. this. happen?

We didn't even know what "this" was, but it was different from anything we had felt before.

We couldn't calm it down, or get our head around it at all, and so finally we called out.

An overnight hospital stay, CT scans, MRIs, EKGs, and several blood tests later, we found out that what was diagnosed as a transient ischemic attack (TIA), or a mild stroke caused by stress, was actually a condition: complex migraines. Just like the sleep issues, skin issues, stomach issues, hair issues, and dental issues before it, the diagnosis was still stress and anxiety.

I'm writing to you right now because if you haven't changed by now, I'm afraid of what else might have been added to this list. And if you have changed only a bit, I'm afraid that this unraveling will only pick up pace if the change isn't *drastic*. Remember what our neurologist said? We picked her specifically because she was a Black woman and the best in her field—and because we knew she would tell us the truth. And she did. Her exact words: "If you want to live, you need to make a drastic change in your life."

Drastic.

Has that happened?

Have you at least told someone else the truth? The container is beyond capacity, and we clearly can't hold all of this truth on our own. We will succumb to it if we try. The truth always needs a resting place or it will lie down wherever it sees fit.

I'm not trying to guilt you. I know guilt causes us more

stress. I'm trying to love on you. Love on us. It's so hard for me to do in the present, but I love what our future holds and I love you and I want it all for you.

You deserve it.

We have said these words to so many Black girls over the years, but now I want to say them to you:

You deserve safety, you deserve protection, you deserve love, you deserve peace.

Breathe, beloved.

Let's do it together, right now.

Breathe in what I'm saying. Breathe out what you are thinking.

We tell the world they don't have to be anything but themselves to be worthy, and then we work until the stress is about to kill us to prove our worth.

It's not just you. It's the paradox of deeply melanated women.

But right now I need you to hear me, because if we are still alive, then there is hope to beat this thing.

I will do my part from where I am. That's the commitment I will make to you. I'm going to start by releasing my fear of the container and beginning to clear it out—carefully. I will rest where the truth rests. And I won't do it in silence or in secret. I promise.

And by the way, if you have done this work already and figured out how to save us, then I just want to say thank you.

I knew we could do it.

With all my love,

Tarana

ACKNOWLEDGMENTS

Thank you.

We want to thank all the contributors, who shared not just their words but their truth, their pain, and their hearts. The phrase "You are your best thing" comes from Toni Morrison's *Beloved*. To all of our amazing contributors and to you, the readers, we wholeheartedly believe that you are your very best thing.

To Toyin Ojih Odutola, thank you for allowing us to use your art on the jacket of this book. Your work embodies the love and humanity that is the core of this work. To Mike and Wendy Hauser at Global Prairie, thank you for being great stewards of the art and designing a cover that captures the spirit of the book.

To Suzanne Barrell, Tati Reznick, Stacy Hollister, Ben Greenberg, Suzanne Gluck, Dorian Karchmar, the Random House team, and the BBEARG team—thank you for your support. This could not have happened without you.

To our families who supported us through all of the writing, chatting, texting, zooming, calling, and editing—we are grateful.

Thanks and love to Sincere, Taylar, and Kaia. Thanks and love to Steve, Ellen, and Charlie.

And one last thing:

Brené: Thank you, Tarana, for trusting me with this work. Thank you for our friendship. I remember when we finally met in person years ago and I kissed you on the cheek. I was just so happy to be with you. I was embarrassed for a split second, but then you kissed me back and we're literally cuddling in all the pictures. I'm grateful for the breadth and depth of our friendship. That we can laugh and talk about decorating and fashion, we can co-create around the difficult and beautiful parts of life, and that we can sing together in the back of cabs.

Tarana: Thank you, Brené. You took a big leap here and I'm so glad you believed we wouldn't fall. You're amazing. So glad to call you friend.

ABOUT THE CONTRIBUTORS

Aiko D. Bethea is a perpetual learner. She co-designs blueprints for folx to create mindsets and spaces where they can thrive. Leadership and organizational development are her favorite wheelhouses. Her greatest space for learning and joy is raising Wes and Ben with their dad extraordinaire.

Austin Channing Brown is a speaker, writer, and media producer providing inspired leadership on racial justice in America. She is the author of the *New York Times* bestseller *I'm Still Here: Black Dignity in a World Made for Whiteness*.

Keah Brown is a journalist, author, and screenwriter. She has been published in *The New York Times, Netflix Queue,* and *Marie Claire* (UK), among other publications. She is represented by Alex Slater of Trident Media Group and Rachel Miller of Haven Entertainment. keahbrown.com

Laverne Cox is a four-time Emmy-nominated actress, an Emmy-winning documentary film producer, and a prominent equal rights advocate and public speaker. Her ground-breaking role in the critically acclaimed Netflix original series *Orange Is the New Black* brought her to the attention of diverse audiences around the world.

Tanya Denise Fields, also lovingly known as Mama Tanya, is the founder and executive director of the Black Feminist Project, the creator and host of Mama Tanya's Kitchen, and the fierce mama bear to six imaginative and precocious children. She lives in the Bronx, New York, with dreams of moving South.

Shawn A. Ginwright, PhD, is one of the nation's leading innovators, provocateurs, and thought leaders on African American youth, youth activism, and youth development. He is a professor of education in the Africana Studies Department and a senior research associate at San Francisco State University.

Prentis Hemphill is an embodiment teacher and founder of the Embodiment Institute (TEI), making connections between healing and our most inspiring visions for social change. Before TEI, Prentis was the healing justice director at Black Lives Matter Global Network. They now host the podcast *Finding Our Way.*

Marc Lamont Hill is the Steve Charles Professor of Media, Cities, and Solutions at Temple University. He is the host of BET News and the author of multiple books, including *We Still Here: Pandemic, Policing, Protest, and Possibility.*

Luvvie Ajayi Jones is a *New York Times* bestselling author, speaker, and podcast host. Her new book *Professional*

Troublemaker: The Fear-Fighter Manual drops March 2, 2021.

Kiese Makeba Laymon is a Black Southern writer from Jackson, Mississippi. Laymon is the author of the novel *Long Division,* the essay collection *How to Slowly Kill Yourself and Others in America,* and the *New York Times* bestselling *Heavy: An American Memoir.*

Tracey Michae'l Lewis-Giggetts is a writer/storyteller and educator whose work explores the intersection of identity and faith/contemplative spirituality. Author of numerous books across several genres, Lewis-Giggetts is also the host of the podcast *HeARTtalk with Tracey Michae'l.*

Kaia Naadira (they/he) is a filmmaker and photographer originally from Alabama. Their photography can be seen in publications like *Salty, Glamour, Les Inrockuptibles,* and *USA Today.* They currently reside in Brooklyn, New York, and are looking forward to the next adventure.

Imani Perry is a professor at Princeton University and the author of six books, including the award-winning titles *Looking for Lorraine: The Radiant and Radical Life of Lorraine Hansberry* and *May We Forever Stand: A History of the Black National Anthem.* Her most recent is *Breathe: A Letter to My Sons.*

Irene Antonia Diane Reece is a contemporary artist and visual activist. Reece is known for her image-based work revolving around the importance of circulating Black family archives. She continues to make work about unlearning white centrism in art, social issues, and community health.

Jason Reynolds is an award-winning and #1 *New York Times* bestselling author. His many books include *Stamped: Racism, Antiracism, and You,* a collaboration with Ibram X. Kendi; *Long Way Down; Look Both Ways;* and the Track series. Most important, he loves his mother.

Yolo Akili Robinson is an award-winning writer, healing justice worker, yogi, and the founder and executive director of BEAM (Black Emotional and Mental Health Collective). His work focuses on creating healing-centered Black communities.

Sonya Renee Taylor is a bestselling author and activist and founder of The Body Is Not an Apology, a digital media and education company exploring the intersections of identity, healing, and social justice using the framework of radical self-love.

Jessica J. Williams is a Black feminist artist and educator dedicated to the creation of authentic and empathetic relationships, communities, and organizations. Her work focuses on empowering individuals—centering the marginalized—in an effort to create inclusive and compassionate communities.

Deran Young is a mom, retired Air Force social worker, and founder of Black Therapists Rock. Her international clinical experience inspires her passion for cross-cultural compassion. She emphasizes communal healing to resolve mental health issues stemming from historical trauma and systemic oppression.

CONTRIBUTOR CREDITS

BACK COVER PHOTO CREDITS

Jason Reynolds: Courtesy of Adedayo "Hype" Kosoko

Austin Channing Brown: Courtesy of Christina Gandolfo

Tanya Denise Fields: Self-portrait courtesy of the author

Kiese Makeba Laymon: Self-portrait courtesy of the author

Prentis Hemphill: Self-portrait courtesy of the author

Tracey Michae'l Lewis-Giggetts: Courtesy of Makayla S. Giggetts

Marc Lamont Hill: Courtesy of dsqphotography.com

Keah Brown: Self-portrait courtesy of the author

Luvvie Ajayi Jones: Courtesy of Kesha Lambert Photography

Shawn A. Ginwright: Courtesy of Takaitheartist

Kaia Naadira: Courtesy of Aziza Fari

Deran Young: Courtesy of Rashid Tillis

Sonya Renee Taylor: Courtesy of Kola Shobu

Irene Antonia Diane Reece: Courtesy of Diego Arrieta

Yolo Akili Robinson: Courtesy of Texas Isaiah

Laverne Cox: Courtesy of Paul Hilepo

Jessica J. Williams: Self-portrait courtesy of the author

Aiko D. Bethea: Courtesy of Nick F. Nelson

Imani Perry: Courtesy of Sameer A. Khan

Toyin Ojih Odutola: Courtesy of Beth Wilkinson

ABOUT THE EDITORS

For more than twenty-five years, cultural worker and organizer TARANA J. BURKE has worked at the intersection of sexual violence and racial justice. Fueled by commitments to interrupt sexual violence and other systemic inequalities disproportionately impacting marginalized people, particularly Black women and girls, Tarana has created and led various campaigns focused on increasing access to resources and support for impacted communities, including the 'me too' movement, which to date has galvanized millions of survivors and allies around the world. Tarana has received numerous accolades and awards for her tireless work, including being named *Time* magazine's 2017 Person of the Year as part of the Silence Breakers, and one of the 2018 *Time* 100 Most Influential People. She has also received the 2019 Sydney Peace Prize, Harvard University's Gleitsman Award, and the Ridenhour Courage Prize.

Twitter: @TaranaBurke

BRENÉ BROWN is a research professor at the University of Houston, where she holds the Huffington Foundation–Brené Brown Endowed Chair at the Graduate College of Social Work. She is also a visiting professor in management at the University of Texas at Austin McCombs School of Business. Brown has spent the past two decades studying courage, vulnerability, shame, and empathy and is the author of five #1 *New York Times* bestsellers: *The Gifts of Imperfection, Daring Greatly, Rising Strong, Braving the Wilderness,* and her latest book, *Dare to Lead,* which is the culmination of a seven-year study on courage and leadership. She hosts the *Unlocking Us* and *Dare to Lead* podcasts, and her TEDx talk, "The Power of Vulnerability," is one of the top five most-viewed TED talks in the world with more than fifty million views. She is also the first researcher to have a filmed lecture on Netflix. *The Call to Courage* special debuted on the streaming service on April 19, 2019. Brené Brown lives in Houston, Texas, with her husband, Steve. They have two children, Ellen and Charlie.

Twitter: @BreneBrown